TOURIST GUIDE TO

KERALA

with Lakshadweep

(The Land of Lavish Lagoons)

SURA MAPS

An imprint of Sura Books (Pvt) Ltd.

(An ISO 9001: 2000 Certified Company)

Chennai ● Ernakulam
Bengalooru ● Thiruvananthapuram

Price: ₹ **70.00**

© PUBLISHERS

TOURIST GUIDE TO KERALA

This Edition	:	February 2011
Size	:	1/8 Demy
Pages	:	136
Code	:	K 4

Price: ₹ 70.00
ISBN: 81-7478-164-1

SURA MAPS
[An imprint of Sura Books (Pvt) Ltd.]

Head Office: 1620, 'J' Block, 16th Main Road, Anna Nagar,
Chennai - 600 040. Phones: 044-26162173, 26161099.

Branches :
- XXXII/2328, New Kalavath Road,
  Opp. to BSNL, Near Chennoth Glass, Palarivattom,
  Ernakulam - 682 025. Phones: 0484-3205797, 2535636

- TC 27/2162, Chirakulam Road, Statue,
  Thiruvananthapuram - 695 001.

- 3638/A, IVth Cross, Opp. to Malleswaram Railway Station,
  Gayathri Nagar, Back gate of Subramaniya Nagar,
  Bengalooru - 560 021. Phone: 080-23324950

Printed at G.T. Krishna Press, Chennai - 600 102 and Published by
V.V.K.Subburaj for Sura Maps [An imprint of Sura Books (Pvt) Ltd.]
1620, 'J' Block, 16th Main Road, Anna Nagar, Chennai - 600 040.
Phones: 26162173, 26161099. Fax: (91) 44-26162173.
e-mail: enquiry@surabooks.com; website: www.surabooks.com

02 11 2000

CONTENTS

1. ALL ABOUT KERALA   1

2. THIRUVANANTHAPURAM
Facts and Figures   13
In and around Thiruvananthapuram   14
Thiruvananthapuram Map   17
Kovalam Map   20
Tourist Information Offices & Accommodation   23

3. KOTTAYAM
Facts and Figures   27
In and around Kottayam   28
District Information Offices & Accommodation   38

4. MALAPPURAM
Facts and Figures & In and around Malappuram   40
Tourist Information Office & Accommodation   42

5. KOLLAM
Facts and Figures & In and around Kollam   43
Tourist Information Offices & Accommodation   48
Ernakulam - Kollam Road, Rail, Waterways Map   49

6. IDUKKI
Facts and Figures & In and around Thekkady   50
In and around Peermedu   52
Kumily, Thekkady Map   53
Munnar Map   55
In and around Munnar   56
Tourist Information Offices & Accommodation   59

7. KOZHIKODE
Facts and Figures & In and around Kozhikode   61
Tourist Information Offices & Accommodation   66
Kozhikode Map   67

8. PATHANAMTHITTA
Facts and Figures & In and around Pathanamthitta   68
Tourist Information Offices & Accommodation   71

9. **ERNAKULAM**
   Facts and Figures & In and around Ernakulam 72
   Ernakulam Map 73
   In and around Kochi 78
   Varkala, Kochi-Fort Map 79
   Tourist Information Offices & Accommodation 81

10. **WAYANAD**
    Facts and Figures & In and around Mananthavady 83
    Tourist Information Offices & Accommodation 86

11. **ALAPPUZHA**
    Facts and Figures & In and around Alappuzha 87
    Tourist Information Offices & Accommodation 90
    Alappuzha Map 91

12. **THRISSUR**
    Facts and Figures & In and around Thrissur 92
    Tourist Information Offices & Accommodation 95

13. **KANNUR**
    Facts and Figures & In and around Kannur 96
    Tourist Information Offices & Accommodation 100

14. **PALAKKAD**
    Facts and Figures & In and around Palakkad 101
    Tourist Information Offices & Accommodation 106

15. **KASARAGOD**
    Facts and Figures & In and around Kasaragod 107
    Tourist Information Offices & Accommodation 110

16. **TRAIN TIMINGS** 112

17. **AIR CONNECTIONS** 124

18. **LAKSHADWEEP**
    Facts and Figures & Tourism in Lakshadweep 126
    Lakshadweep Islands Map 129
    Package Tours 130
    Tourist Information Offices & Accommodation 132

All about Kerala

A Bird's Eye View of Kerala

Facts and Figures

Capital	:	Thiruvananthapuram
Area	:	38,863 Sq.kms.
Population	:	3,18,38,619 (2001 census)
Density of Population	:	819 per sq. km.
Length	:	575 Km
Language	:	Malayalam
Literacy	:	90.92%
Sex Ratio	:	(Females per 1000 males) 1058
Temperature	:	21°C to 35° C
Monsoon	:	June to September /October
Tourist Season	:	November to April
Seaports	:	Kochi, Vizhinjam, Neendakara and Beypore
Time	:	GMT + 5:30
Currency	:	Indian Rupee
Climate	:	Tropical
Names of Districts	:	Thiruvananthapuram (Trivandrum),Kollam, Alappuzha (Alleppey), Pathanamthitta, Kottayam, Idukki, Ernakulam, Thrissur (Trichur), Palakkad (Palghat), Malappuram, Wayanad, Kozhikode (Calicut), Kannur (Cannanore), Kasaragod
Major Cities	:	Thiruvananthapuram, Kochi (Ernakulam district) and Kozhikode.
Taluks	:	61
Revenue Villages	:	1452
City Corporations	:	5
Grama Panchayat	:	991
Block Panchayat	:	152
District Panchayat	:	14

Airports	:	Thiruvananthapuram, Kochi and Kozhikode.
Road and Rail	:	The state is well connected by rail and road.
Seaports	:	Major: Kochi
		Minor: Beypore (Kozhikode), Alappuzha, Kollam
Major Beaches	:	Kovalam, Varkala, Fort Kochi, Kappad and Bekal
Major Wild Life Sanctuaries	:	Thekkady (Periyar), Parambikkulam, Wayanad Silent Valley, Aralm, Peechi-Vazhani, Chimani, Shenduruny, Idukki, Chinnar, Peppara, Neyyar.
Bird Sanctuary	:	Thattekad, Kumarakom
Major Hill Stations	:	Ponmudi, Peermedu, Thekkady, Munnar and Wayanad
Farm/Cash Crops	:	Rubber, Coffee, Tea, Spices, Pepper, Cashew, Coconut, Arecanut and rice
Exports	:	Marine, Coir, Handicrafts, Spices, Food and other products
Major Industries	:	Tourism, Information Technology, Fertilizer, Oil Refining and Power Generation, Ship Buildings, Machine Tools, Electronics, Cables, Rubber

Kerala, one of the southern States of India is situated along the gregarious shores of the Arabian Sea at an expanse of about 38,863 Sq. Km. The entire State has been known since time immemorial, among myriad other features, for its inherent tranquillity. Although keeping pace with the present day advancements, Kerala remains unscathed by the modernisation.

Kerala is endowed with various landscapes and natural resources. The western ghats, thick forests, palm-fringed lakes, rivers, lagoons etc. are to name a few. The coconut farms of Kerala are world renowned. It is no surprise that a domain of such a rich heritage fostered the growth of religion, culture and art.

All the major religions co-exist harmoniously in Kerala in as much as it is no exception to following the ideal of secularism of the nation - India, of which it is a part. Here temples greet mosques, mosques wish churches and churches welcome temples. Ancient temples, mosques and churches are dissipated all over the State. The synagogues stand tall as reminiscences of the ancient Jewish settlers. It was here that the famous dance drama 'Kathakali' evolved from an ancient form of Sanskrit drama called "Kudiyattam". It has been a centre of Sanskrit, the language of Indian culture. "Silapathikaram", an ancient marvellous Tamil literary work of perpetual glory cites evidences of the "Kudiyattam" having been in vogue here for more than 20 centuries.

The State, much longer than it is wide, is about 580 km. in length and is flanked by Karnataka in the north and the north-east and Tamil Nadu on the east and the south. The western ghats, with an average height of 900 mts and peaking from 1800 mts to 2400 mts at places, run all along the eastern border of the State, thus forming a natural cordon. The highest South Indian Mountain peak known as the **Anamalai Peak** which is about 2689 mts in altitude is situated here in Idukki district. Kerala, the smallest of the South Indian States, makes up to 1.3 per cent of the total area of the nation.

History has it that Kerala has been an irresistible temptation to visitors right from the ancient times. Here, phoenicians had traded in ivory spices and peacocks as long back as 3000 years ago. Many historic visitors to Kerala have adored its indisputable greatness in ways which came to them naturally.

Behold! a few of such historic utterances.

"When you leave the islands of Seilan and sail westwards about 60 miles, you come to the great province of Malabar which is styled India the greater. It is the best of all the Indus and is on the main land... There is in the kingdom a great quantity of pepper and ginger and cinnamon and nuts of India".

- Marco Polo in his books of Travels (1292 AD)

"We next come to Kalikat, one of the great ports of the district of Malabar and in which merchants from all parts are found. They put a thief to death for stealing a single nut or even a seed of any fruit; hence thieves are unknown among them. The greatest part of Mohammedan merchants of this place are so wealthy that one of them can purchase the whole freightage of such vessels as put in here.

- Sheik Ibu Batuta (1342-47 AD)

"Such security and justice reign in Malabar that rich merchants bring to it from maritime countries large cargoes of merchandise which they disembark and deposit in the streets and market places and for a length of time leave it without consigning it to any one's charge or placing in under guard".

- Abdur-r-Razzak (1442 AD)

"There was one point in regard to the inhabitants of Malabar, on which all authorities, however diametrically opposed to each other on other points agreed and that was with regard to the independence of mind of the inhabitants. This independence of mind was generally diffused through the minds of the people."

- Lord William Bentinck (1804 AD)

"Some of the more remarkable of the vegetable and the animal productions of the Malabar Coast have been known to the Western Nations from times antecedent to Christian era, and have been the objects of maritime enterprise and commerce through all the succeeding centuries".

- *William Logan (1887 AD)*

While high mountains form the border on one side of the State, the deep blue Arabian Sea does on the other. And obviously there is no scarcity for beaches. The beaches here are quite different from most of those at other places since what gives them the border lining for a length, longer than one's imagination, is lavish palmgroves. This enthralling uniqueness add to the beauty and attract a lot of visitors. Some of the famous beaches in the State are at Kovalam, Papanasam (Varkala) Shanghumugam, Vizhinjam, Alleppey Kappad, Bekal and Payambalam.

The mountains have gentle contours and rounded tops and sharp peaks are hardly seen. This is a characteristic of the Himalayas. The mountain range is a treasure from tip to toe as the tops are covered with evergreen forests while all along the incline are valuable teak, rich plantations of cardamom, tea, rubber, coffee and pepper. The southwest monsoon, between May and August, fetch more shower than its ironical rival, north-east, in October. The heavy downpour and the broken terrains give rise to a number of rivers and brooks whose beauty has besotted many a visitor.

Naturally enriched with minerals Kerala has an abundance of 'Monazite' on its beaches which is converted into a radioactive material called 'thorium' used as an atomic fuel.

In the retrospect, Kerala has been ruled over by a number of dynasties. It had been under the empire of Ashoka in the 3rd century BC. Then the historic battles had continually placed it under the control of several heroes. The rulers of the three great Tamil dynasties viz., the Cheras, the Cholas and the Pandyas had succeeded in turns, to bring the coveted region under their belts. Then the Islamic emperors conquered it and then it went to the hands of Vijayanagar Kingdom which offered resistance to the iconoclastic approach of the Muslim rulers.

People

Exotic, about the people of the State is their classification and the factors upon which it is based.

The sect of people who have devoted themselves to religion and vedic practices, popularly known as the Brahmins is called Nambudris: They excel in Sanskrit studies and are patrons of a number of fine arts.

Wielding their swords and shielding their sods in the hierarchical era were the sect known as the Nairs who have thereafter taken to various other occupations. They adhere to the joint family traditions with an unrelenting family bondage. The oldest male member of the family, the 'Karnavar', is looked upon with reverence by the rest of the family.

Reference to Mahatma Gandhi's words "India lives in Her villages" seems imminent looking at the 'Thiyas or Ezhavas'. They are traditionally the cultivating class engaged in coconut farms.

Among others are a large number of Hindu class distributed all over the State. These include several hill tribes, Uralis, Ullatans and Mudrans.

The Christians again in several classes and groups, have their indispensible contributions to the greatness of the State in the field of 'Education', 'Industry' and 'Economic development'.

'Moplas' as are called, the Muslims of Kerala are an industrious lot, their main occupation being trade. However, Kerala also hosts a small colony of Jews.

Culture

Kerala has established its name in the fields of music, dance, architecture, painting and other forms of artistic expression.

Malayalam, the vernacular of the region, rich in its literature, has imbibed vocabulary to a substantial extent from the ancient and yet not obsolete language, Sanskrit. The translations of the Ramayana, the Mahabharatha and the Bhagavata (from Sanskrit to Malayalam) by Ezhuthachan in the 16th century are still adored by the pious people. Thus it has been a land of a number of genii in almost all the fields.

Dances of Kerala

Kathakali

Kerala owes its transnational fame to this nearly 300 years old classical dance form which combines facets of ballet, opera, masque and the pantomime. It is said to have evolved from other performing arts like *Kootiyattam, Krishnanattam* and *Kalarippayattu*. Kathakali explicates ideas and stories from the Indian epics and Puranas.

Presented in the temple precincts after dusk falls *Kathakali* is heralded by the *Kelikottu* or the beating of drums in accompaniment of the *Chengila* (gong). The riches of a happy blending of colour, expressions, music, drama and dance is unparallelled in any other art form.

Oppana

A dance form essential to the wedding entertainment and

festivities of the Malabar Muslims. Maidens and young female relatives sing and dance around the bride, clapping their hands. The songs of *Mappilappattu,* are first sung by the leader and are repeated by the chorus. The themes are often teasing comments and innuendoes about the bride's anticipated nuptial bliss. *Oppana* is often presented as a stage item today.

Krishnanattam

A spectacle for both the scholar and the simple rustic. The visual effect is enhanced by varied and colourful facial make-up with larger-than-life-masks, made of light wood and cloth padding, for certain characters. The characters who do not wear masks have specific facial colours applied within the frame of a white chutti. The predominant colours used are dark green, flesh tint and deep rose. Most of the characters wear red vests and flowing *'Uthariyams'*. The characters of *Krishna, Arjuna* and *Garuda* wear dark blue vests.

The traditional performance lasts for eight days and covers the whole span of *Krishna's* life from his birth to *'Swargarohanam'* or ascension to the heavens.

Orchestral accompaniments are *Maddalam, Ilathalam* and *Chengila.*

Mohiniyattom

The sinuous dance of the enchantress, this is a distinctive classical dance form of Kerala. Slow, graceful, swaying movements of the body and limbs and highly emotive eye and hand gestures are unique to this dance form. The simple, elegant gold-filigreed dress, in pure white or ivory, is akin to the traditional attire of the women of Kerala.

This dance was adopted by the Devadasi or temple dancers, hence also the name 'Dasiattam' which was very popular during the Chera reign from 9th to 12th century.

Kakkarissi Natakom

Kakkarissi natakom is a satirical dance-drama based on the puranic legends of *Lord Siva* and his consort *Parvati* when they assumed human forms as *Kakkalan* and *Kakkathi* - a nomadic tribe of fortunetellers. The language is a blend of Tamil and Malayalam. The chief characters are *Kakkalan, Kakkathi, Vetan, Velichappadu, Thampuraan* and the ubiquitous Jester. The *Dholak, Ganchira, Chenda* and the *Harmonium* provide the background score.

Thiruvathirakali

Thiruvathirakali is a dance performed by women, in order to attain everlasting marital bliss, on *Thiruvathira* day in the Malayalam month of *Dhanu* (December-January). The dance is a celebration of marital fidelity and the female energy, for this is what brought *Kamadeva* (the god of love) back to life after he was reduced to ashes by the ire of Lord Siva. The sinuous movements executed by a group of dancers around a *nilavilakku*, embody 'lasya' or the amorous charm and grace of the feminine. The dance follows a circular, pirouetting pattern accompanied by clapping of the hands and singing. Today, *Thiruvathirakali* has become a popular dance form for all seasons.

Kolkkali

A folk art mainly of the agrarian classes, *Kolkkali* is a highly rhythmic they never miss a beat. In Malabar, *Kolkkali* is more popular among Muslim men.

Thullal

Thullal is a solo performance combining the dance and recitation of stories in verse. This satiric art form was introduced in the 18th century by the renowned poet Kunchan Nambiar.

Humour, satire and social criticism are the hallmarks of *Thullal*. The make up, though simple, is very much akin to that of *Kathakali*. The Thullal dancer is supported by a singer who repeats the verses and is accompanied by an orchestra of *mridangam* or *thoppi maddalam* (percussions) and cymbals. There are three related forms of Thullal - *Ottanthullal* , *Seethankanthullal* and *Parayanthullal* - of which the

7

first is the most popular. The three are distinguished by the costumes worn and the metre of the verses.

Kootiyattom

Muslims of Malabar. *Duffmuttu* is staged as a social event during festivals and nuptial ceremonies.

Kootiyattam literally means "acting together". This is the earliest classical dramatic art form of Kerala. Based on Sage Bharatha's *'Natyasasthra'* who lived in the second century, *Kootiyattam* evolved in the 9th century AD.

Kootiyattam is enacted inside the temple theatre, there are two or more characters on stage at the same time, with the *Chakkiars* providing the male cast and the *Nangiars* playing the female roles. The *Nangiars* beat the cymbals and recite verses in Sanskrit, while in the background *Nambiars* play the *Mizhavu,* a large copper drum.

The Koodal Manickyam temple at Irinjalakkuda and the Vadakkunnatha temple at Thrissur are the main centres where *Kootiyattam* is still performed annually. Ammannoor Madhava Chakkiar is an unrivalled maestro of this rare art.

Duffmuttu

Duffmuttu is also known as *Aravanamuttu.* It is a group performance popular among the

The artistes beat on a quaint round percussion instrument called the *Duffu,* the leader of the group sings the lead, while the others form the chorus and move in circles. The songs are often tributes to martyrs, heroes and saints.

Duffmuttu can be performed at any time of the day and has no fixed time limit.

AYURVEDA

The traditional form of medicine and treatment is yet another feather to the hat. 'Ayurveda', the English for which is 'Knowledge of life' has flourished here since very ancient times. 'Ayurveda', the system of treatment believed to be older than 5000 years is based on the philosophy, "Prevention is better than cure". However, it offers a lasting cure to patients suffering from various diseases.

It is not only a system to cure diseases but the system teaching us how to achieve 'Perfect Health' for diseased or abnormal conditions and how to lead our life, both physical and mental, to attain the bliss of real life.

It is almost as old as mankind and at the same time so new as modern man that no disease is there which is incurable or uncontrollable unless missed too much.

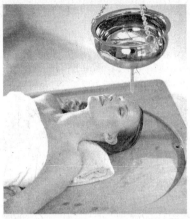

According to ayurveda, human body is composed of three fundamental elements called 'Doshas' - which represent the physico-chemical and physiological activities of the body, 'Dhatu' which denotes the materials entering into the formation of a basic structure of the body cell, thereby performing some basic actions and 'Malas' the substances which are partly used in the body and partly excerted in yet another form after serving their physiological activities.

'Doshas' are three - *vata, pitta,* and *kapha* and they may not be equal and same in all. According to the dominance of each dosha every man is categorised to different types.

Physical and mental co-operation of the patient to make necessary changes in his life style and food habits also are essential to attain the natural dynamic balance of the doshas and once that balance is maintained the illness is gone.

It describes how to live to avoid disease in each climate and how can perfect health be maintained throughout the life. Ayurveda has a separate branch called 'Rasayana' to maintain youth and vitality to recover lost health in diseased conditions.

In Ayurveda, all treatment is aimed at building up the strength of the person which would help him to lead a health and happy life.

Methods of Ayurvedic treatment are primarily classified into three.

1. *Antharparimarjanam*
2. *Bahirparimarjanam*
3. *Sastrapranidhanam*

It lays more emphasis on the promotion of positive health and prevention of diseases.

Yoga and Tantra which are primarily meant for spiritual attainments have also certain prescriptions for the prevention and cure of psychic, somatic and psychosomatic ailments.

The unique features of Ayurveda treatment of medicine are:

1. Treatment of individual as a whole, ie. not only the condition of other parts of his body but also the condition of his mind and soul.

2. Medicines are available on reasonable prices.

3. No import involved ie. medicines are vegetables, metals, minerals and animal products which are available in nature.

BOAT RACES

In the months of August and September, over hundred thousand men and women gather on the banks to witness a spectacular water regatta **the Snake Boat Races**. The most famous one is the

Nehru Trophy Boat Race which began in 1952 on the occasion of the visit of India's first Prime Minister, Jawaharlal Nehru to Alappuzha. It is now a major event held on the second Saturday of every August and features the gigantic snake boats of Kerala, the Chundans - once the battleships of the Malayalee King of Yore. Now, the boat race has grown as most important tourist even with boats being sponsored by different villages. Another traditional boat race, Champakulam Moolam Vallam Kali is connected with a temple festival. There are other snake boat races too.

The chief competitors of the trophies are *Champakulam, Kavalam, Karichal, Jawahar Thayangari, Kallooparamban, Pulinkunnu, Nadubhagam, Cheruthana, Kandangari and Paippad.*

AMUSEMENT PARKS

The first theme park in India is **Essel World** in Mumbai established in 1981. But now, South India itself has more than twelve such parks.

Fantasy Park: It is the first amusement park in Kerala located at Malampuzha in Palakkad district. Entree fee is separate for each items. (Address: Fantasy Park, Malampuzha, Palakkad. Ph: 0491-2815122, 2815123). Fax : (0491-2815124)

Veega Land: It is located 12 km from the Ernakulam bypass (Kakkanad route).

Time: 10.30 am - 6.30 pm on weekdays. 10.30 am - 9.30 pm on weekends and holidays. Address: Veega Land, Pallikkara,Kakkanad,

Kochi-683 565. Ph: 0484-2684001, 2684002.reception1 @veegaland.com

Silver Storm: This park is situated 19 km from Chalakudy in Trissur district. Address: Silvern Storm, Athirappally Road, Vettilappara, Chalakudy, Trissur - 680 721. Ph: 0488-2769116.

Dream World: It is located near Chalakudy on way to Atirappally and Vazhachal falls. It is 8 km from the town. Address: Dream World, Athirappally Road, Kanjirappalli, Chalakudy, Trissur-680 721. Ph: 0488-2766935, 2766955, 2767665. www.dreamworldkerala. com

RIVERS AND BACKWATERS

There are forty four rivers in Kerala. Out of 44 rivers, forty one rivers are west flowing and 3 are east flowing rivers which cut across Kerala with their innumerable tributaries and branches. It turn into rivulets in

summer.

The backwaters from a specially attractive and economically valuable feature of Kerala. The biggest backwater is the Vembanad Lake which opens out into the

Arabian Sea at Cochin port. The other important backwaters are Veli, Kadinamkulam, Anjengo, Edava, Madayara, Paravoor, Ashtamudi, Kayamkulam, Kodungallur and Chetuva. The deltas of the rivers interlink the backwaters and provide excellent water transportation.

Festivals

When one thinks of the festivals of Kerala, the one that spontaneously springs to the mind is **'Onam'**, though there is a long list of others too! It marks the beginning of the new year in the Kerala's aboriginal calendar. It falls in the month of August-September which is called the month of Chingom. It is obviously celebrated with enthralling pomp and show.

'Ammankudam', Arattu', Chandankudam, 'Chuttuvilakku,' Ezhunallathu', 'Pallivetta', 'Paraveppu, 'Pongala', 'Seeveli',

Thalappoli', 'Velichappadu' (Komaram) are some of the unique Hindu rituals, performed regularly with fabulous fanfare apart from the festivals like Diwali, Dasara etc.

The Christian festivals, the **Christmas**, the Good Friday and the Easter are cherished with equal zeal and zest all over the State and the Ramadan and the Bakrid bring about no less joy to the people of Kerala.

TOURISM ADMINISTRATORS

Sri. Kodiyeri Balakrishnan
Minister for Tourism,
Government of Kerala,
Room No.216, III Floor,
North Sandwitch
Block, Secretariat
Thiruvananthapuram - 695001

Phone: 91-471-2327976, 2327876
Sri. Dr. Venu V, IAS
Secretary (Tourism)
Government of Kerala
Government Secretariat
Thiruvananthapuram - 695001
Phone: 91-471-2332632
Fax: 91-471-2518977

Sri. M. Sivasankar, IAS
Director (Tourism)
Phone: 91-471-2322547
Fax: +91-471-2322279

VELI TOURIST VILLAGE
2 kms from Thiruvananthapuram Airport. This village is a delightful waterfront park which has become extremely popular with Trivandrumites.

Thiruvananthapuram

Facts and Figures

Area : 2,192 Sq.kms. ● Population : 2,105,349 (2001 census) ● Headquarters : Thiruvananthapuram ● Tourist Season: September to May.

Thiruvananthapuram is the State capital. Trivandrum Central Railway Station and Central Bus Station is at Thampanoor. It has rail links with Bangalore and Chennai. Fine roads branch out of the city connecting it to all southern parts of India. Trivandrum Airport (International) linked by flights to Cochin, Chennai, Delhi, Goa and Mumbai. International flights also operate to Colombo, Male, Dubai, Abudhabi, Kuwait and Singapore.

Bounded on the east and north east by the mountain ranges of Western Ghats, in the South by the fertile rice bowl district of Kanyakumari presently in the State of Tamil Nadu and on the west by the Arabian Sea. The hillocks stand majestically right on the shore (Arabian Sea) as though beckoning to the sea and hence the rains run down the hills caressing every inch of the incline, to the sea. The city has a lot to offer to the voracious eyes of the tourists. The modern style of architecture seems to compliment the antique monuments.

Tourists' Interest

Sri Padmanabha Swamy Temple: It is situated in the heart of the city. It would rather be more pertinent to say the city had been built around the temple as it is

believed to have come into existence on the first day of 'Kaliyuga' era, (28-12-3101 BC). The presiding deity is, as the name implies, Lord Padmanabha, one of the variations of Lord Vishnu. The deity can be seen reclining on serpent 'Anantha'. The 'Dharshan' (reverential sight) can be had through three doors, the face through south door, the navel through the middle and the feet through the North. This venue is one of the exquisite group of 108 Temples dedicated to 'Maha Vishnu'. Two festivals are held annually. Only Hindus are allowed inside the temple. Wearing of shirt or any attire to cover the upper part of the body by MEN inside the temple premises is strictly prohibited. Thus men are restricted to 'Dothi' (Pants not allowed) and women to sarees and blouse. (Chudidhar, pants, shirts etc. not allowed).

Dharshan

Hours   : 04:15 - 05:15 hrs,
                06:45 - 07:30 hrs,
                08:30 - 11:15 hrs,
                11:45 - 12:00 hrs,
                17:00 - 18:15 hrs,
                18:45 - 19:30 hrs.

Sri Subramaniyaswamy Temple - Ullur: This temple dedicated to Lord Subramaniya (Murugan) is situated 7 kms from Thiruvananthapuram.

Bhagawathy Temple - Attukal: Located 2 km from the State capital is this temple dedicated to Goddess Bhagawathy. The famous 'Pongala Utsavam' popularly known as 'Attukkal Pongala' lasts for 10 days.

Sarkaradevi Temple - Chirayinkeezhu: This temple is, again, dedicated to Goddess Bhagawathy. It is situated 18 km from Thiruvananthapuram. Bharani Utsavam - a 10 day festival Kaliyoothu Mahotsavam - a folk ritual are celebrated annually.

Siva Temple, Aruvippuram: The idols in this temple were installed by Sri Narayana Guru. 'Sivarathri' festival, during which devotees observe fast and forgo the night's sleep and perform puja (offer prayers and worship) and adore Lord Siva, is famous here.

Thiruvambadi Sri Krishna Temple, Varkala: Sri Krishna, one of the 10 'Avathars' (Divine incarnations) of Lord Vishnu is the presiding deity. It is located at Manthra near Varkala. A festival to mark the birthday of Lord Krishna is celebrated here, in a grand manner.

Kuthiramalika (Puthenmalika) Palace Museum: At a stone's throw from Sri Padmanabha Swamy temple this marvellous specimen was built by Maharaja Swathi Thirunal Balarama Varma. The workmanship, traditional style typical of Travancore Architecture, captivating wood carvings and the importance given to every minute detail of the construction, all reflect the grandeur of the construction techniques of the olden times. The 'Maharaja' (King) was himself a great poet, musician, social reformer, and statesman. In the palace to be seen are breathtaking paintings and invaluable collections of the royal family.

Visiting
Hours   : 08:30 - 13:00 hrs,
                15:30 - 17:30 hrs,
                Closed on Mondays.

Entrance Fee:
Adults   : Rs. 10/-
Children   : Rs. 3/-
Foreigners   : Rs. 20/
Camera permit   : Rs.15/-
(Outside)
Video   : Rs.500/-

In and around Thiruvananthapuram

Thirunavaya: Overseeing the gushing river Bharatapuzha is the historical city of Thirunavaya. This city was the ancient venue for an exotic festival called 'Mamankam'.

It is apposite to call it the 'Sport of Kings' for this festival was indeed a stiff contest between the rulers of various parts of Kerala to declare the emperor among them. The last 'Mamankam' was celebrated in the year 1755. The place can also be reached from Tirur in Malapuram district which is about 8 km away.

The Government Art Museum (The Napier Museum): Built in the year 1880 by an English architect

in honour of Lord Napier, Governor of Madras, this museum is situated on the crest of the public gardens near the observatory hills. The structure has a built-in natural air-conditioning system and a good collection of archaeological and historic artefacts, bronze idols, ancient ornaments, a temple chariot, ivory carvings, sculptures, models and zoological specimens. A clock about 4 centuries old and a cot made out of herbal wood for the king are among those exclusive ones. The zoological gardens with beautiful meadows and attractive landscapes surround the structure. The use of plastic in the museum premises is prohibited.

Visiting Hours : 10:00 - 16:45 hrs, closed on Mondays and forenoons of Wednesdays.

Sree Chithra Art Gallery: Within the periphery of the compound of Napier Museum is yet another piece of beauty to behold - Sree Chithra Art Gallery. It contains a large collection of paintings of various Indian and South Asian Schools. There is a good number of paintings of the veteran, Raja Ravivarma - a name worshipped by many artists. Copies of Kerala's exquisite murals, paintings of the Rajput, Mughal and the Tanjore Schools, reproductions of murals of Ajantha, Bagh, and Sittannavasal, paintings from China, Japan, Tibet and Bali - all add to the decorum. The canvases of Roerichs, vividly capturing the colours of the Himalayas, can also be seen.

In a nutshell, it is a visual banquet to any pair of connoisseur's eyes.

Visiting Hours : 10:00 - 17:00 hrs, closed on Mondays and forenoons of Wednesdays.

Entrance Fee:

Adults : Rs. 10/-
Children : Rs. 4/-

Veli lagoon: The seemingly placid sheet of water that backed away from the visibly reverberant sea offers a general idea of the famous backwaters of Kerala. Boating facilities are also available. Pedal boats, row boats and motored boats are available on hire. Children, in particular have a lot of fun and frolic climbing over the huge sculptures which dot the landscapes, and riding a ferry.

Visiting Hours : 08:00 - 18:00 hrs
Boat Rentals : 10:00 - 17:30 hrs

Rate Tariff :

Safari boat	-	Rs.10/-(per head)
Speed boat	-	Rs. 120/-
Pedal boat (4 seater)	-	Rs.50/- (for half an hour)
Pedal boat (2 seater)	-	Rs.40 (for half an hour)

The Public Park: The public park encompasses some vital attractions like the zoo, the botanical gardens and the observatory atop a hill, popular as 'observatory hill'.

The Zoological Park: This is one of the pioneer zoos in India, located amidst a wonderful botanical garden. The tall, huge and massive trees, wild bushes, shrubs and lawns, the lake strewn with wild fowls and mild ducks give the visitors a glimpse of the jungle in the city. Different varieties of snakes, poisonous and non-poisonous, inherently active and sluggish can also be seen.

Visiting Hours : 09:00 - 18:15 hrs, closed on Mondays.

Entrance Fee:
Adults   : Rs. 10/-
Children   : Rs. 5/-
(from 5 to 12 yrs)
Camera Permit   : Rs.25/-

The Connemara Market: This is the city's colourful market forum. Its grandness is overt from the archway entrance near the Secretariat and is often a tourists' hang out. Hence everything from 'A' to 'Z' is available in this market.

The Observatory: On the top of the observatory hills at the vantage point, 60 mts above the sea level which is also the highest point in the city, the observatory, carrying out extra-terrestrial observations, offers to the visitors, a panoramic view of the city.

The Kanakakunnu Palace: The palace and its vast grounds provide the stage for many cultural meets and programmes.

The Science and Technology Museum Complex: The museum contains articles of science and technology, modern and old, including all branches of science. Educative, informative and interesting as it is to the young and old alike, it inculcates a quest for science and a passion for technology in the young minds.

Visiting Hours : 10:00 - 17:00 hrs closed on Mondays
Entrance Fee : Adults - Rs.2/-, Children Re. 1/-.

Shanghumukham Beach: 8 km off the city, abutting Thiruvananthapuram airport and Veli tourist village, this beach is the ideal spot for watching Sunset. The glorious sight of the mighty Sun submerging into the conspicuously endless expanse of the blue waters in the faraway horizon sending out His golden yellow and orange rays is relished, time and again, by visitors of all sorts. Those who are looking for a diversion or a relaxation can just step into the recreation club at the beach. A gigantic sculpture of a mermaid, 35m long can also be seen apparently in the posture of taking a well deserved rest after a tiring swim. A huge starfish, several times bigger than the ones found in the sea made not of flesh and skin but of bricks and concrete but there is a restaurant for the visitors to satisfy their hunger. The 'Chacha Nehru Traffic Training Park', here, helps children learn the traffic rules.

Priyadarshini Planetarium: The planetarium helps the viewers get a glimpse of the magnificent extraterrestrial happenings beyond the average human perception.

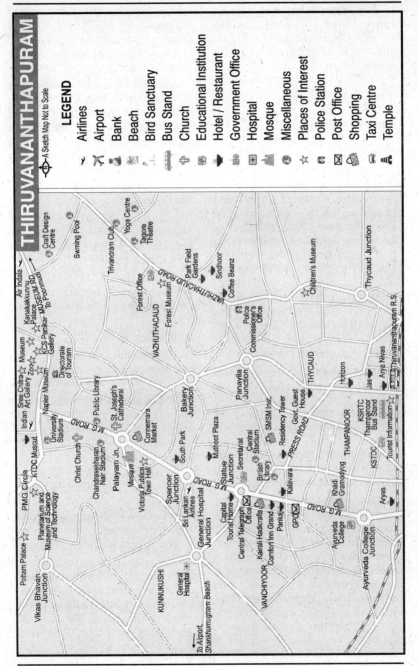

THIRUVANANTHAPURAM

LEGEND

A Sketch Map Not to Scale

- Airlines
- Airport
- Bank
- Beach
- Bird Sanctuary
- Bus Stand
- Church
- Educational Institution
- Hotel / Restaurant
- Government Office
- Hospital
- Mosque
- Miscellaneous
- Places of Interest
- Police Station
- Post Office
- Shopping
- Taxi Centre
- Temple

The show takes the viewers light-years into the incomprehensible space. They are sure to loose themselves in the narration and the movements of the replica of the heavenly bodies on the dome shaped screen overhead.

Show Schedule: 10:30, 12:00, 15:00 and 17:00 hrs
Entrance fee : Adults - Rs.15/-
Children - Rs.10/-
(from 3-10 yrs)

Chacha Nehru Children's Museum: The museum is named after the first Prime Minister of India, late, Sri Jawaharlal Nehru. It is well known that he doted on children and even a quick glance through his biography would reveal many an incidence that alludes to this fact. And quite rightly the museum is intended for kids. It has a large collection of dolls (nearly 2000), stamps and masks.

Visiting Hours: 10:00 - 17:00 hrs, Closed on Mondays

The Secretariat: This is an edifice of the Roman architectural style. The government administration is carried out here. The offices of ministers and bureaucracy are also present.

The Kerala Legislature Complex: Complex, as is the construction of auditoriums with minimal noise levels, optimum feed back etc., meticulous care has been exercised in maintaining the acoustic properties of the hall with advanced acoustic treatments and latest sound system technologies. Though equipped with modern facilities, the structure bears a resemblance to the classical form of grand architecture with its dome-tower, carved galleries and the ornamental work on the teakwood panel and the ceiling.

Akkulam Tourist Village: This is a picnic-makers' paradise. Boating is popular here. Children love the spot and it is always seen swarming with children revelling in joy. There is also a swimming pool to add to the fun.

Visiting Hours : 10:00 - 19:00 hrs
Boat Rentals :
(Open 10.00 - 18.30 hrs)
Safari boat-Rs.250/- for 21 persons
Pedal boat - Rs.60/- for 4 persons
Row boat - Rs.40/-

Children's Park -
Visiting Hours : 10:00 - 19:30 hrs
Entrance fees : Adults - Rs.5/-
Children - Rs.3/-

Swimming pool -
Visiting Hours : 06:00 - 18:30 hrs
Entrance fees : Adults - Rs.20/-
Children - Rs.10-

Thiruvallam: It is situated 10 km off the city. Canoeing is popular in the calm stretch of backwaters between Thiruvallam and Kovalam.

Lord Parasuraman's Temple is here by the river at Thiruvallam, Chithranjali, the State Film Development Corporation's studio is at Thiruvallam.

Aruvikkara Dam: This beautiful dam is just a half an hour's drive from the city, 16 km away. It is situated on the banks of the river Karamana. A temple dedicated to Goddess Durga can also be seen. A stream near the Temple is abundant in fish that dauntlessly near the shore to be fed by the visitors. The visitors seem to enjoy feeding them too.

The Kovalam Beach: A half-an-hour drive from the city covering 16 km leads to this Nature's marvel of international acclaim. It has been a tourists' favourite since long past. Visitors from all over the globe throng to the resort and spend days together trying to grab every bit of the joy it proffers. There are also three crescent beaches; the most popular being the southernmost known as the 'light house beach'. Accommodation is available. Boarding and lodging is available at different rates to cater to the needs of all the visitors. Kovalam offers a variety of activities including snorkelling, catamaran rides, sunset viewing, cycling on the beach etc.

Vizhinjam Rock Cut Cave: 17 km from the city, it takes about half an hour to reach the spot. The awe-inspiring cave temple here comprises of splendid sculptures cut out of rocks in the 18th century A.D. The cave encloses a one-celled Shrine with a loose sculpture of Vinandara Dakshina-murthi. The outer wall of the cave depicts half complete reliefs of Lord Siva with His consort Goddess Parvathi. In short, it is a place to admire and worship.

The Koyikkal Palace - Nedumangad: Situated at the place called Nedumangad 18 kms from the city which is again around half an hour's drive it is also enroute to the Ponmudi hill station and the Courtallam Waterfalls. This ancient palace dates back to the 15th century. The traditional 'Nalukettu' building here is two storeyed with inclined gabled roofs, an inner courtyard and museums of folklore and numismatics set up by the department. 'The Folklore Museum' established in 1992 is a treasure house of quaint musical instruments, occupational implements, household utensils, models of folk arts, etc.

The Numismatics Museum houses rare and historically valuable coins evidencing the trade relations of the State.

Sri Mahadeva Temple: It is believed that this temple dedicated to Lord Siva, located at Kazhakuttom, had been built in the 14th century. Mitramanda-puram Temple is another old temple and is situated on the outskirts of the city.

Neyyar Dam: It is a picnic spot about 29 km from the city. There is a watch tower. Just as crocodiles are attracted to the water, the visitors are attracted to the crocodile farm, here. The majestic 'King of the forest' - Lions can be sighted on a safari in the 'Lion Safari Park'. There is also a deer park. And there are also boating facilities at the reservoir.

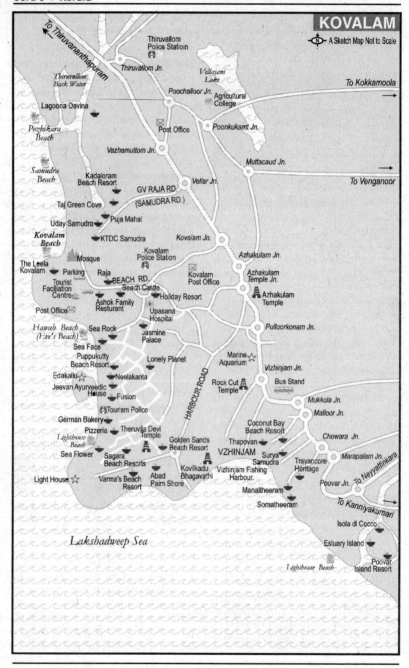

KOVALAM

A Sketch Map Not to Scale

To Thiruvananthapuram

Thiruvallom Police Statioin

Thiruvallom Jn.

Vellayani Lake

Poochalloor Jn.

Agricultural College

To Kokkamoola

Thiruvallom Back Water

Lagoona Davina

Pozhikara Beach

Post Office

Poonkukamt Jn.

Vazhamuttom Jn.

Samudra Beach

Kadaloram Beach Resort

Vellar Jn.

Muttacaud Jn.

To Venganoor

GV RAJA RD. (SAMUDRA RD.)

Taj Green Cove

Uday Samudra

Puja Mahal

KTDC Samudra

Kovalam Jn.

Kovalam Beach

Mosque

Azhakulam Jn.

The Leela Kovalam

Parking

Raja

Kovalam Police Station

Azhakulam Temple Jn.

Tourist Faciliation Centre

BEACH RD.

Beach Castle

Kovalam Post Office

Azhakulam Temple

Post Office

Ashok Family Resturant

Holiday Resort

Upasana Hospital

Pulloorkonam Jn.

Hawah Beach (Eve's Beach)

Sea Rock

Jasmine Palace

Sea Face

Puppukutty Beach Resort

Lonely Planet

Marine Aquarium

Vizhinjam Jn.

Edakallu

Jeevan Ayurveedic House

Neelakanta

Fusion

Rock Cut Temple

Bus Stand

Mukkola Jn.

German Bakery

Tourism Police

Malloor Jn.

Lighthouse Beach

Pizzeria

Theruvila Devi Temple

Coconut Bay Beach Resort

Chowara Jn.

Sea Flower

Sagara Beach Resorts

Golden Sands Beach Resort

Thapovan

VZHINJAM

Surya

Samudra

Travancore Heritage

Marapalam Jn.

To Neyyattinkara

Light House

Varma's Beach Resort

Abad Paim Shore

Kovilkadu Bhagavathi

Vizhinjam Fishing Harbour.

Poovar Jn.

Manaltheeram

Somatheeram

To Kanniyakumari

Isola di Cocco

Lakshadweep Sea

Estuary Island

Poovar Island Resort

Lighthouse Beach

Varkala: Situated 40 km from the city, this seaside resort is a spa and an important Hindu pilgrim spot. Near here, stands the hill Sivagiri on the top of which Sri Narayana Guru, a great social reformer had spent his last days. The coastline is famous for its high cliffs and mineral springs. The 2000-year-old Sri Janardhana Swamy Temple, a century old tunnel and a Nature Cure Centre are the main attractions here.

Peppara Wild Life Sanctuary: This sanctuary occupies over a 53 sq. km of the western ghats and is about 50 km from Thiruvananthapuram, on the way to Ponmudi. It is rich in flora and fauna. It also has wide-spread hillocks, forests and eucalyptus plantations. It is a never-to-miss spot for every wildlife enthusiast.

Ponmudi : About 54 km from Thiruvananthapuram, this hill resort is about 915 mts above sea level. The pathways are narrow. The atmosphere is cool, the

ground is lush green and the place is woody. The air is filled with the fragrance of mountain flowers. Exotic butterflies can be spotted. Springs and small rivulets are enchanting and enlivening.

There is a deer park close by and there are also excellent trekking trails. There is also a KTDC restaurant and a government guest house.

Accommodation : Guesthouse : Cottages & Rooms Rs.430-1100/- (4 bed) Dormitory Rs.800/-.

For reservations contact: The Secretary, General Administration Department (Political), Govt. Secretariat, Thiruvananthapuram.

The Padmanabhapuram Palace: On the way to Kanyakumari, 63 km from Thiruvananthapuram is the place called Tuckalai in which stands the magnificent palace which had been the abode of the hierarchical rulers of Travancore. This is a well preserved wooden palace and a standing testimony to the traditional Kerala school of architecture. The extraordinary murals, exquisite floral carvings and the black glossy granite floor have withstood the test of time. The palace remains closed on Mondays.

Agasthyakoodam: It is a part of the Sahyadri range of mountains and is the second highest peak in Kerala at a height of about 1890 mts above sea level, the highest one being Anamalai (2689 ft). These mountains are covered with thick forests which provide home to a large number of wildlife species. Agasthyakoodam is abundant in rare medicinal herbs with amazing curative properties. Brilliantly hued orchids and a variety of plants are also found in large numbers. Home to certain birds and a seasonal dwelling to a huge set of certain migratory ones; this mountain attracts professional as well as occasional birdwatchers. This legendary mountain can also be accessed on foot from Kotoor, near Neyyar dam and also from Bonacaud. The ideal season for trekking is from December to April. Trekkers need to obtain a forest pass from the wildlife warden, Forest Department, PTP Nagar, Thiruvananthapuram.

Somatheeram: Somatheeram is also known as 'The Tropical Garden of Eden'. It is an Ayurvedic Beach resort which preserves the age old heritage of Kerala. It is 21 kms. from Thiruvananthapuram and 9 kms. south of the Kovalam Beach. Somatheeram, 15 acres of green garden terraced heights sloping down to the sandy beach stretching to the tranquil, turquoise sea changing colour and mood momentarily as the white clouds sail past over it.

Somatheeram has an Ayurvedic Centre, where several rejuvenative therapies based on the Vedic science Ayurveda are undertaken.

Ayurvedic treatment with herbal preparations directed towards strengthening the immune system, preventing curing diseases without any side effects. Somatheeram Ayurvedic Hospital and Yoga Center has been selected for the Award of Excellence in the category of Best Ayurvedic Centre.

Manaltheeram Ayurvedic Beach Village: Manaltheeram is a picturesque beach resort and near to Somatheeram Beach Resort.

Festivals

India is known for Her festivals. Thiruvananthapuram as all other parts of India celebrates a number of festivals almost all through the year though they occur in a quicker succession in one part of the year than the other.

Christmas, Easter, Good Friday are celebrated with much fanfare by the Christian community here and the exchange of greetings and wishes among the Christians and their Hindu and Muslim brethren, is a commonsight.

Muslims, have their heyday during Bakrid and Ramadan. The air is filled with serenity as they observe fasting during Ramadan month. The celebrations are coupled with piety and stoicity. Warm greetings exchange kind hearts regardless of religion or caste.

Hindus make merry of a number of festivals. Apart from the functions like Diwali, Dasara. etc. which are celebrated with equal pomp and show throughout the Nation and with hearty greetings, gifts and wishes being conveyed among kith and kins and to the friends belonging to other religions, with equal zest, there are a few unique to the State.

Onam: This is celebrated in the months of August-September. It commemorates the reign of the legendary king Mahabali in the Hindu Mythology.

One week is earmarked for tourism during the peak of the festive season to enable the tourists as well as the inhabitants to move about and have their slice of the hilarity.

Arattu: Vetta and Arattu occur twice a year. Holy processions are held from Sri Padmanabha Swamy Temple to Shangumugam Beach led by the members of the royal family of erstwhile Travancore.

The idols from the Temple are taken to the sea for a holy dip. Cultural performances including the Kathakali are part of the celebrations.

Attukal Pongala: Thousands of female devotees throng the 'Bhagawathy Amman' Temple at Attukal, just a couple of kilometers from Thiruvanantha puram, for the 10 day Pongala festival. As it is a 'Ladies' Special' festival, men are not supposed be in the proximity. 'Pongala', considered to be the Goddesse's favourite, is in fact a kind of sweet porridge. The long line of women absorbed in devotion, preparing this ritual offering can be seen all the way till the East Fort and farther.

Chandanakudam Mahotsavam: This is a colourful Islamic festival. Devotees bring offerings in the form of money in pots decorated with flowers and incense sticks and sandalwood paste sending out their sweet aroma, to the tomb of an austere lady, Bee Umma, at Beemapally, near Thiruvanantha-puram.

Nishagandhi Dance and Music Festival: The 'Nishagandhi Open Air Theatre', Kanakakunnu Palace, Thiruvananthapuram hosts this festival of Indian classic dance and music from the 22nd to the 27th of February every year. The evenings are filled with, Bharathanatyam, Kathak, Kathakali, Kuchipudi, Manipuri, Mohiniattam, Odissi and traditional dance forms of classical music and Jugalbandi, etc.

Gramam: This is a 10 day (Jan. 14-23) village fair along the beach at Kovalam. The venue is provided by the quadrangular penthouse courtyard with an open centre, called the Nalukettu. Arts and Crafts fair, Kathakali, Thiruvathirakali, Mohiniyattam, Oppana Kalaripayattu, Theyyam Kumettikali, Kakkarisi Natakam, Panchavadyam, Chakyarkoothu, Ottanthullal, etc. deserve special mention.

Flavour Food Festival: Celebrated from 5th to 11th April by renowned hotels across Kerala at the Kanakakunnu Palace Grounds, Thiruvananthapuram, this festival is the time for various cuisines of the world, titillating dishes and inviting delicacies.

Tourist Information Offices

* **Tourist Facilitation Centre**, Department of Tourism, Park View. ✆:91-471-2321132
* **Tourist Information Centre**, Railway Station, Thampanoor. ✆: 91- 471- 2334470
* **Tourist Information Centre**, KSRTC Central Bus Station, Thampanoor. ✆: 91- 471- 2327224

- **Tourist Information Centre,** Domestic Airport. ℂ:91-471-2501085
- **Tourist Information Centre,** International Airport. ℂ:91-471-2502298
- **Tourist Facilitation Centre,** Kovalam. ℂ:91-471-2480085
- **District Tourism Promotion Council (DTPC),** Vellayambalam. ℂ:91-471-2315397 Fax: 91-471-2313606

Accommodation

Thiruvananthapuram (STD: 0471)

- **The Muthoot Plaza,** Punnen Road, Thiruvananthapuram-695 039 ℂ: 2337733; Fax: 2337734; Email: tvm@muthootplaza.com
- **Hotel Saj Lucia,** East Fort, Thiruvananthapuram-695 023. ℂ: 2463443; Fax: 2463347; Email:sajlucia@md2.vsnl.net.in
- **Surya Samudra Beach Garden,** Heritage, Pulinkudi, Mullur P.O., Thiruvananthapuram-695 521; ℂ: 2480413, 2267333, 2481825; Fax: 2267124; Email: reservations@suryasamudra.com
- **Best Western Swagath Holiday Resort,** Kovalam, Thiruvanantha-puram-695 527 ℂ: 2481148/49; Fax: 2481150; Email: swagat. resort@gmail.com
- **Hotel Chola International, Aristo Junction,** Thampanoor, Thiruvananthapuram ℂ: 2334334, 2334601-04; Fax: 0471-2473172
- **Hotel Kadaloram Beach Resort,** G.V. Raja Road, Kovalam, Thiruvanathapuram-695 527 ℂ: 2481116-20; Fax: 0471-2481115; Email: kadaloram@vsnl.com

- **Samrat Hotel,** Thakaraparambu Road, Thiruvananthapuram-695 023 ℂ: 2463314, 2463214, 2460167; Fax: 0471-2570432
- **Hotel South Park (4 Star)** ℂ: 2333333 Fax: 2331861 Email: reservations@southpark.com
- **Hotel Luciya (4 Star)** ℂ: 2463443 Fax: 2463347 Email:sajluciya@md2.vsnl.net.in
- **Horizon (3 Star)** ℂ: 2326888 Fax: 2324444 **Email**: hotel horizon@asianetindia.com
- **Hotel Pankaj (3 Star)** ℂ: 2464645 Fax: 2465020
- **Mascot Hotel (3 Star)** ℂ: 2318990 Fax: 2317745 mascathotelthiruvandapuram @kerala.com
- **Jass** ℂ: 2324881 Fax: 2324443 Email:jas@md2. vsnl.net.in
- **Ariya Nivas** ℂ: 2330789 Fax: 2330423 www.ariyanivas. com/ index.html
- **Residency Tower** ℂ: 2331661 Fax: 2331311 Email:rtower@ md2.vsnl.net.in
- **Chaithram** ℂ: 2721243/ 2721245 Fax: 91-0471-2721249 Email:corporate@ktdc.com
- **Geeth** ℂ: 2471987 Fax: 2460278
- **Oasis** ℂ: 2333223 Fax: 2328054
- **Paramount Park** ℂ: 2323474 Fax: 2331311
- **Prasanth** ℂ: 2316189 Fax: 2316407
- **Thampuru** ℂ: 2321974 Fax: 2321987
- **Hotel Pallava** ℂ: 2452839
- **Amritha** ℂ: 2323091 Fax: 2324977
- **Navarathna** ℂ: 2330473
- **Regency** ℂ: 2330377 Fax: 2331690 **Email**:hotelregency @satyam.net.in

- Jacobs Hotel ✆: 2330052
- Aulakam Hotel ✆: 2330488
- Hotel Silver Sand ✆: 2460318 Fax: 2478230
- Moon Light ✆: 2551186
- Hotel Highland ✆: 2333200 Fax: 2332645
- Keerthi ✆: 2325650 Fax: 2325792
- President Hotel ✆: 2313228 Fax: 2330305
- Safari ✆: 2477202
- Yathri Niwas ✆: 2324462
- Hotel Kyvalya ✆: 2330724 Fax: 2334176
- Sukhwas ✆: 2331967

Kovalam *(Beach Destination)* **(STD: 0471)**

- Hotel Ashok (5 Star) ✆: 2480101 Fax: 2481522 Email: htlashok@giasmd01.vsnl.net.in
- Lagoona Beach ✆: 2480049 Fax: 2462935 Email:davindia@ hotmail.com
- Surya Samudra ✆: 2480413 Fax: 2481124 Email:reservation @suryasamudra.com
- Bethsaida ✆: 2481554 Fax: 2481554 Email:saturn@md3. vsnl.net.in
- Uday Samudra ✆: 2481654 Fax: 2481578 Email:udaykov@md4. vsnl.net.in
- Manaltheeram Beach Resort ✆: 2268610 Fax:2267611 Email:somatheertham@vsnl.com
- Nikkis Nest ✆: 2481822 Fax: 2481182 Email:nest@ giosmd01.vsnl.net
- Somatheeram Ayurvedic Beach Resort ✆: 2268101 Fax: 2267600 Email: @somatheeram.in
- Hotel Sea Face ✆: 2481835 Fax: 2481320 Email: seaface@sancharnet.in

- Hotel Samudra ✆: 2480089 Fax: 2480242 Email:samudra@ md3.vsnl.net.in
- Bright Resorts ✆: 2481190 Fax: 2481210 Email:bright@ md3.vsnl.net.in
- Coconut Bay ✆: 2480566 Fax: 2343349 Email:cocobay@ vsnl.coms
- Ideal Ayurvedic Resort ✆: 2268632/2268396 Email: idealresort@eth.net
- Hotel Neelakanta ✆: 9847875206 Fax: 2485180 Email:hotel neelakanta@yahoo.com
- Santhatheeram ✆: 2481972 Fax:2481972 Email:sntheeram @ md4.vsnl.net
- Sea Rock ✆:2481721 Fax: 2480422
- Hotel Rockholm ✆: 2480606 Fax: 2480607 Email:rockholm@ techpark.
- Hotel Aquarious ✆: 2481072 Fax: 2481072 Email:vunus@ md3.vsnl.net.in
- Beach and Lake Resort ✆: 2382086 Fax: 2382086 Email: beach@beachandlakeresort.com
- Hotel Aparana ✆: 2480950
- Hotel Blue Sea ✆: 2480401
- Raja Hotel ✆:2480355 Fax: 2480455
- Moon Light ✆:2480375 Fax: 2481078
- Neptune Hotel ✆:2480222 Fax: 2460187 Email:replica@ vsnl. com
- Wilson Beach Resort ✆:2210019 Email:wilson@md3. vsnl.net.in
- Hotel Seaweed ✆: 2480391 Fax: 2722698 Email:seaweed@ in3.vsnl.net.in

- **Merriland Tourist Home** ℂ: 2480440 Fax: 2481456 Email:kovalam@md3.vsnl. net.in
- **Hilton Beach Resort** ℂ: 2484077 Fax: 2481476
- **Golden Sand** ℂ: 2481476 Fax: 2481476
- **Hotel Orion** ℂ: 2480999 **Email**: orionbeachresort@hotmail.com
- **Jeevan House** ℂ: 2480662 Fax: 2480662 **Email**:kovalam@md3. vsnl.net.in
- **Royal Retreat Cottage** ℂ: 2481080/2484060
- **Hotel Thushara** ℂ: 2480692 Fax: 2481693 **Email**:hushara@md3. vsnl.net.in
- **Hotel Thiruvathira** ℂ: 2450588
- **Golden Sands** ℂ: 2481945/ 2481476
- **Sandy Beach Resorts** ℂ: 2480012 **Email**:sandybeach @vsnl.net.in
- **Hotel Palmshore** ℂ: 2481481 Fax:2480495 **Email**: abad@vsnl.com
- **Varmas Beach Resorts** ℂ: 2480478 Fax: 2480578 **Email**:ushas@ md4.vsnl.net.in
- **Hawah Beach Hotel** ℂ: 2480431 **Email**:topic@md3.vsnl.net.in
- **Pappukutty** ℂ: 2480235 Fax: 2480234
- **Lobster House** ℂ: 2480456
- **Sea Flower Home** ℂ: 2480554 Fax: 2481069
- **Holiday Home** ℂ: 2480497
- **Hotel Deepak** ℂ: 2480667
- **Swagath Resorts** ℂ: 2481148 Fax: 2481150 **Email**:yajkal@ md2.vsnl.net.in

Travel agents, Kovalam: Western Travel Service ℂ: 2481334. Elite Tours & Travels ℂ: 2481905, 2481405. Universal Travel Enterprises, ℂ: 2481729. Visit India, Lighthouse Road, ℂ: 2481069. Banyan Tours & Travels, ℂ: 2481922. Great Indian Travel Service, Lighthouse Road, ℂ: 2481110.

Convention Centre: ITDC, Kovalam ℂ: 2480101.

Cultural Centre, Kovalam: Ayyipilla Asan Memorial Kathakali School.

Two Wheeler Hire, Kovalam: Voyager Travels, Near Police Station, ℂ: 2481993, Fax: 2451858.

Varkala *(Beach Destination)* **(STD: 0472)**

- **Taj Garden Retreat (4 Star)** ℂ: 2603000 Fax: 2602296 Email:retreat.varkala@tajhotel.com
- **Hill Top** ℂ: 2601237 Fax: 2601237 **Email**:kutty@ techpark. net
- **Sea Pearl** ℂ: 2660105 Fax: 2605049 **Email**:seapearl@md3. vsnl.net.in
- **Preeth** ℂ: 2600942 Fax: 2600942 **Email**:preethonline @sathyam.net.in
- **Thiruvambadi** ℂ: 2601028 Fax: 2604345
- **Skylark Cliff Beach Resort** ℂ: 2602107 Fax: (0473) 2601311

Kottayam

Facts and Figures

Area : 2,203 Sq.kms.
• Population : 19,53,646 (2001 census) • Headquarters : Kottayam • Tourist Season: September to March.

About 154 kms in the Northwest of Thiruvananthapuram and about 64 kms in the Southeast of Kochi spanning the foothills of the unrelenting range of gigantic mountains, the Western Ghats, stands the city of Kottayam with its captivating mangrove forests, lush green paddy fields and a generous expanse of coconut groves rightly punctuated by enthralling brooks amidst teeming white lilies. Among the agricultural produce of the place are cashcrops like rubber, tea, pepper and cardamom. No wonder that a place of such picturesque beauty with tall trees, wide area and so on forms the natural habitat for scores of birds. There are many places which would interest tourists of varied tastes.

The religious harmony of the district can be sensed from the presence of over 50 Temples, 70 Churches and several Mosques including the one 1000 years old. It is also the gateway to a number of pilgrim centres like Sabarimala, Mannanam, Vaikom, Ettumanoor, Bharananganam, Erumeli, Mannarkad, Aruvithura, Athirempura, Perunna Vazhapalli and Thrikkodithanam near Changana-chery.

Air: The nearest international airport is at Nedumbassery, Ernakulam, 90 km North.

Ferry Station: Boats are available here to Alleppey, Nedumudi, Kumarakom and Kavalam.

Tourist Interest

Mahadeva Temple: This Temple, situated in the busy area of Kottayam is dedicated to Lord Siva. The legend has it that the idol here is 'Swayambu' (Self-manifested) and not installed. A 12 day festival is celebrated annually.

Sri Krishnaswamy Temple: Just 8 km from Kottayam, this temple is famous for the festival, Ezhunallathu procession in which Elephants have their own part to play along with humans. The festival goes on for 10 days and so does the ritual procession. Kathakali, Ottamthullal and other classical art forms of Kerala come alive during the festival.

Bagawathy Temple: About 6 km from Kottayam is the place called Kumaranallur where this temple stands with the architecture of the 'Gopurams' (Temple-Tower, Portal Tower) of Tamil Nadu. The idol is made of 'Anjanakkal' (antimony sulphate) and a 9 day festival is held every year.

Dakshina Mookambika Saraswathy Temple: This temple dedicated to Goddess Saraswathy-the Goddess of Arts and Learning and the consort of Lord Brahma - the God of Creations, is situated 10 kms from Kottayam at Panachikkadu in Chingavanam. The nine day festival 'Navarathri' (nine nights) is famous here.

Mahadeva Temple: Ettumanoor, 12 km north of Kottayam, is where this temple is dedicated to Lord Siva is situated. Here, the deity is in two forms, Vallya (Love) and Rudhra (Fury). The mural paintings of the temple especially that of Nataraja on the 'Gopuram' (Tower) and the ezharaponnana (7½ Elephants finished in gold) are famous. The festival 'Ezhara-ponnana Ezhunallathu' lasts for 10 days in February/March.

St. Mary's Church: Situated at Mannarkad, 8 kms from Kottayam, this church is dedicated to St.Mary. This is one of the most important churches of the Malankara Jawbite Syrian Christians. The 'Ettunompu', a festival of fasting for 8 days is held annually during which devotees from far and wide pour in to take part in rituals and prayers.

St. Mary's Ferona Church: About 20 km from Ettumanoor, this church at Bharananganam, is one of the oldest churches in Kerala. The feast of carmel and that of St. Sabastian are held, annually.

Panchalimedu: Situated 7 km from the Mundakkayam - Kuttikanam stretch on the Kottayam-Kumili road lies Panchalimedu, at an attitude of about 2500 feet above the sea level. A three hour trek from Valliankavy, which is connected by bus service from Kottayam takes you to the spot. According to legends, the *Pandavas* stayed here and the pond beside a small temple is where *Panchali* is said to have bathed.

Kesari Falls: The Kesari Falls otherwise known as *Valanjamakanam Falls* lies in between Kuttikanam and Murinjapuzha on the Kottayam-Kumili route. Valanjamakanam is a three-hour journey from Kottayam by any bus to Kumili.

In and Around Kottayam

Kumarakom: The breath-taking beauty of the mangrove forests, the green sea of paddy fields and the vast, fantastic coconut groves benevolently accommodating eye-pleasing and thirst-quenching rivulets, canals, channelled between wild flora and mild lilies extend a warm welcome to every nature-loving tourist. The resorts nearby offer comfortable accommodation and exclusive leisure options like an ayurvedic massage, yoga, meditation, boating, fishing, angling and swimming. This place is 10 km from Kottayam on the Eastern bank of Vembanad lake.

The Vembanad Lake: This lake at about 16 km from Kottayam is the repository to myriad rivers, rivulets and canals of Kottayam. This enchanting tourist spot is fast turning out to be known also as a backwater tourism destination. The fish-rich lake offers excitement not only to fishing hobbyists but also to boating maniacs. The sights here are to be seen and enjoyed. House boat cruises and holiday packages are offered by the Kumarakom Tourist Village. The placid lake turns vibrant with the arrival of Onam as it is the place for spectacular regatta (the snake boat races)

Kumarakom Bird Sanctuary: About 16 km from Kottayam, on the banks of the splendid lake of Vembanad is this ornithologists'

lure - the bird sanctuary where a number of species of birds flock in and flock out during migration. Popular among the migratory birds are Siberian stork, egret, darter, heron and teal. Some of the other common varieties are woodpecker, skylark, crane, waterhen and parrots. Taking a cruise on the Vembanad lake, the curious visitor, could catch a glimpse of a few of the endless species of living flying machines whose mysteries have been puzzling expert ornithologists across the globe ever since the study began. Pathiramanal, an enchanting island can be reached by boat.

Visiting Hours : 06:00 - 18:00 hrs

Tariff for Houseboat cruises

One day cruise on full board basis: Single apartment houseboat for 2 persons - Rs.5,000/-

Twin apartment for 4 persons including food - Rs.6,000/-

One night, 2 days cruise on full board basis: Single apartment houseboat for 2 persons - Rs.12,500/- Twin apart houseboat for 4 persons including food Rs.14,500/-

Stationary houseboat on room only basis: Single apartment houseboat for 2 persons - Rs.1195, twin apartment houseboat - Rs.995/= (per apartment)

For reservations please contact: KTDC Kumarakom Tourist Village, Kavanattinkara Ph. : 2525861, Central Reservation, KTDC, Mascot Square, Thiruvananthapuram. Phone: 2316736.

Pathiramanal: Pathiramanal, which means sands of midnight, is a wonderful island on the backwaters. According to mythology a young Brahmin once, dived into the Vembanad lake to perform his evening ablutions and the water made way for the land to rise from below to form this

3

beautiful island which is now the abode of a variety of migratory birds from different parts of the world. The area of the island is about 10 acres.

Nattakom and Panachikad Reservoirs: In the lush green environ, the marvellous reservoirs add lusture to the calm village. The landscape here again is an invitation to scores of migratory birds. The boat ride from Kodoorar in Panachikad to Kumarakom is very popular. Other interesting features are Ayurvedic massages, boating, fishing and swimming.

Vaikom Tourist Land: This piquant picnic spot is ideal for langorous break. Various recreations including boat cruises on the Vaikom lake are on offer.

Mannanam Tourist Home: It is 8 km from Kottayam. It sites the St. Joseph's Monastery associated with the name of Fr. Kuriakose Elias of Chavara (1805-71). One of the saintly figures of the Syrian Catholic Church of Kerala. An intricate network of shimmering waterways embroider the richly green landscape, making the place ever so charming. There are boat cruise packages, ingenuously devised to make the tourists' experience most exciting. Through the Pennar canal, the cruise does not forsake the scenic backwaters of Alappuzha and Ernakulam.

Anchuvilakku: Anchuvilakku, meaning five lamps where five is the English for 'Anchu' and lamp for 'Vilakku' was built near the boat landing pier at Changanacheri by the great freedom fighter 'Veluthampi Dalawa'. He was also the one who established the Changanacheri market, one of the largest in Kerala. Five lamps are lit on this stone lamp post using kerosene. It is 22 km from Kottayam.

Nadukani: A fabulous hill-top-spot with abundant stretches of beautiful meadows and gigantic tenacious rocks is this place Nadukani which offers a overall view of the immensely beautiful land lying below.

Aruvikkuzhi Waterfalls: 18 km. from Kottayam and 2 km along a narrow muddy terrain this spot of boundless charms receives visitors looking for sheer enjoyment. The awe-inspiring streams jink their way through the benign landscape and the gushing waters cascade down the mountains with relentless fury and fall with a majestic roar from a height of 100 ft. The enormous rubber plantations here provide shade for Sun-beaten tourists.

Kariambukayam: The glorious Manimala river embellishes the elegant spot, Kariambukayam, Meloram in between the panchayat jurisdictions of the town known for its plantations Kanjirapalli and the pilgrim spot Erumeli. Enriched with rich natural features, the place has quite a few reservoirs on which, at occasions, aqua banquets are organised. The natural reservoirs and waterfalls at Melaruvithodu on the

Ernakulam-Thekkady road play a substantial part in glorifying Kottayam.

Erumeli: 'Unity in Diversity', one of India's hallmarks, is well evident here as thousand upon thousands of Hindu pilgrims, fasting and observing strict austerity for a specific number of days, traditionally worship and offer prayers at a Mosque in Vavarambalam, on their way to Sabarimala which is another pilgrim spot. The mosque is dedicated to 'Vavar' a thick crony of Lord Sree Ayyappa, the presiding deity of Sabarimala.

Erumeli, the village with a natural bliss is situated 60 km South-east of Kottayam.

Maniamkunnu: The tenacious mountains characterised by wild plants and trees, shrubs and bushes, exotic flowers prudently part at places giving rise to astounding valleys of natural splendour. The higher the mountains soar the deeper the valleys dive.

Kayyoor: The ghat region with its own aspects of natural charms, and blanketed by lush green hilly vegetation is the pride of the Bharanganam panchayat in Kayyoor. A temple dedicated to the Pandava brothers (5 sons of the couple King Pandu and Kunthi in the legendary epic 'The Mahabharatha') is also found here. The temple lamps are lit only with ghee as in the temple at Sabarimala. Women are not allowed inside the temple.

St. Mary's Church: At Bharananganam, the church dedicated to St. Mary entombs the mortal remains of the benedicted Alphonsa and is now a popular pilgrim centre where multitude of devotees throng during the festival called the 'Feast of the Blessed Alphonsa' which is held in the month of July every year.

Illaveezhapoonchira: 'The valley where leaves do not fall' is what the very name of the domain means as it is devoid of trees. The startlingly beautiful valleys of here spanning over thousands of acres contribute in great deal to the natural attractions of Kottayam. The four distinct mountains soaring to heights of around 3200 ft, completely green deserve special mention. The valleys look entirely different when the gracious rains fill them up to form awesome lakes. This is one of the ideal spots to watch both Sunrise and Sunset. Thus the place offers dawn to dusk enchantment. Accommodation is provided by a DTPC rest house nearby.

Kannadipara: This place derives its name from the exotic rocks it possesses. 'Kannadi' which means mirror and 'para', 'rock' have merged together to christen the unique place whose rocks shine and reflect the Sun like mirrors. It is also the highest point in Ilaveezhapoonchira. Pazhakakanam plateau through which the resplendent river Kadapura flows is about 3 km from here. The place is rich in bamboo grooves, captivating meadows and eyecatching wild flora. The Kazhukankulimali waterfalls, here, as though tired of its long trek down the unyielding mountains thuds into the river below. To the east of the place, steep rocks enclose a natural fort.

Mankallu Mudikal: There are three magnificent hills in the region which are not too faraway from one another. Verdant and flat landscape marks the hilltops. An areal view of the place reveals a cauldron like formation. The place has no trees on the hilltops.

Illickal Mala: This mountain peak, soars to about 6000 ft above sea level. A lot of typical mountain streams, apparently emerging from the oblivion, merge merrily with one another to give rise to the all but calm Meenachil river. Here, the tranquil atmosphere, sought-after solitude, gentle breeze, picturesque environs and an endless list of natural features make the region all the more salubrious. Reaching the hilltop calls for a trek of about 3 km up the hill which will get amateurs a feel of mountaineering.

Illickal Kallu: This mammoth hill is made of three distinct hills averaging about 4000 ft and above, above the sea level. These hills or rocks are named after their own strange countenance. The umbrella shaped rock, locally called 'Kuda Kallu' resembles an umbrella. Among other common and rare herbs, a medicinal herb called the 'Neela Koduveli' which is, according to a common belief, blessed with paranormal powers

to yield a rich harvest, is seen in large numbers here. 'Kunnukallu' which means hunch-back rock has a hunch on its sides. The supposedly ominous bridge of just about ½ a metre is called 'Narakapalam' which means 'bridge to hell'. The sight of Sunset and Moonrise, partially simultaneous happenings on fullmoon days is simply astonishing on the hilltops. The thin thread like lining of blue beauty, seen from the hilltops, at a faraway horizon is indeed the vast Arabian Sea.

Ayyapara: This spot extends to about 20 acres in area and is about 2000 ft in altitude. The legend says that 'The Pancha Pandavas' the five Pandava brothers, sons of King Pandu and his spouse Kunthidevi spent certain number of days here during their tenure of exile. It is also believed that the name of the place was originally, 'Anchupara', meaning five rocks and has later become to be known by the present name as time rolled by. However, some attribute the name to the temple dedicated to Lord 'Ayyappa' here. Four sturdy pillars support the rock-roof of the Temple. The mountain and every part of the nature here condition the wind into a pleasantly cool breeze. There is also a cave which can hold upto 15 persons. This is also a spot to admire Sunset.

Kolani Mudi: This is also one of the extravagant peaks, with an inviting cave, in the seemingly limitless range of Ilaveezhapoonchira mountains.

Marmala Stream: This is a place of streaming enjoyment. The startlingly beautiful stream leads to a roaring waterfalls, squired by the jungle around. The water falling from a height of about 200 ft. after taking an arduous course along the hillocks has with meticulous care and an architectural expertise, sculpted on the rocks down below a deep pond whose beauty speaks for itself. The natural bridge right under the waterfalls is yet another example of natural splendour.

Vazhikkadavu: The all but calm Meenachil river flows on one side of a medley of hills and rocks on the suburbs of the main district. This hill station comprises huge rocks, magnificent and elegant. The extremely tall rocks on one side of the main rock form spine-chilling abyss. Come December and January, the entire region is invaded by flora and fauna, the eyecatching colours and orchids, and so are the onlookers.

Kurisumala: This is a popular pilgrim centre of the Christians, about 3 km from Vazhikadavu. During and after the Holy week the place is filled with thousands of devotees, their souls soaked in faith, carrying small wooden 'Holy Crosses' up the hill in awesome reverence to the Almighty and offer prayers while the air is filled with divinity. There is also a Holy Monastery of the Jews atop the hill. The eastern side of the hill

known as the 'Murugamala' has to its pride a temple dedicated to 'Lord Muruga' the son of 'Lord Shiva' in Hindu Mythology. The enchantment seems to begin the moment one sets off on the road to Kurisumala as the houses of European style alongside the path and an artificial lake, both designed by the famous architect, Larie Baker are sights never-to-miss.

Thangalappara: Situated near the resplendent hill resort of Karuthikallu and the alluring Kottathavalam, this is a Holy place of Islamic pilgrimage as it is here that the mausoleum of Sheikh Fakruddin is located.

Kottathavalam: This is another place of archaeological interest as the legends allude that the royal family from the town of Madurai in Tamil Nadu, rested here on their way to Poonjar. A magnificent cave which can be reached by the rock cut steps near the Murugamala, is an addition to the natural attractions. The cave contains rock cut chairs and couches and carvings of the figures of Goddess Madurai Meenakshi, Lord Ayyappa, Lord Muruga and the legendary personality known for her chastity, Kannaki and also the weapons and armoury.

Poonjar Palace: This palace stands tall as a genuine repository to a rare and a large collection of regal antiques, pristine artifacts, extraordinary furniture etc. A fabulous palanquin, a 'Thoni', made out of a single piece of quality wood ad hoc for 'Ayurvedic' massages, a hanging light with arms for holding lamps, traditional palm leaf scriptures, decorated jewel boxes, sculptures of Lord Nataraja, the dancing form of Lord Siva, grain measures of the olden days, statues and armoury are to name a few.

As part of an annual ritual, a conch is taken on a procession. At a stone's throw from the palace, there stands a temple identical to that of Madurai Sri Meenakshi. The wall sculptures tell stories from the Puranas. Another temple in the proximity is the 'Sastha Temple' dedicated to Lord Ayyappa in which a rare row of stone wall lamps known as the 'Chuttuvilakku' is famous.

Vagamon: Situated on the border of Kottayam and Idukki, this place is the breeding centre of 'Kerala Livestock Board'. This is again a typical hill station with bountiful tea-gardens and stimulating meadows.

The greatest attraction of the place in Kurishumala, a sky scraping mountain with a small church on its peak and the Kurishumala Ashramam, a monastery atop another hill.

Pala, Kanjirapally, Vayaskara and Chirattamon: The two former towns are known for their rubber plantations watered by the generous rivers Meenachil and Manimala. The later two, house 'Ayurvedic Rejuvenation Centres'.

St. Mary's Church: Located at Cheriapalli, 2 km from Kottayam town, this church of splendid architectural value, dedicated to St.Mary, is the result of coalition of the Kerala and Portuguese styles. Built by Thekkumkoor Maharajah it dates back to the year 1579. The wall paintings reveal general themes and the ones relating to the Holy Bible.

Thazhathangadi Valiapalli: About 2 km on the west of Kottayam town, this ancient church of the 1550's stands as a living monument of the Knanaya Orthodox Syrian Community. The Persian Holy Cross here is believed to be one of the seven brought by St. Thomas Pahlavi inscriptions can also be found.

There is yet another structure of ancient glory. A Holy Mosque, believed to be of the last millennium is also seen here.

Dharmasastha Temple: Dedicated to Lord Ayyappa at Pakkil, about 3 km from Kottayam. This temple is one of the eight established by Parasurama the legendary founder of Kerala. 'Sankranthi Vaibhavam' - an annual festival in which a fair of household articles comes up is celebrated in the month of June and July.

St. George's Church: This church situated at Puthupalli, believed to have been built by the rulers of Thekkamkoor has a famous golden cross. An annual festival known as the feast of St. Geroge (Gee Varghese), is famous.

Siva Temple: This temple at Thalikkotta, 2 km from Kottayam, is dedicated to Lord Siva. The royal families of Thekkamkoor have worshipped here. Sivarathri festival in January-February and another 10 day festival in April-May are held here.

The CSI Cathedral Church: This church was built over 175 years ago during the British rule of India.

Syrian Churches: The Old Seminary, Marthoma Seminary and Vadavathoor Seminary and the Malankara Orthodox Syrian Church headquartered at Devalokam, Kottayam are places of historical, architectural and devotional interests.

St. Thomas Mount: 1200 ft. above sea level, where exclusive view of the Vaikom lake and its extraordinary surroundings are in the offing, is a Holy place of worship and prayer for the Christians.

Siva Temple: Located at Vaikom 40 km from Kottayam,

this temple dedicated to Lord Siva has a rich architecture typical of Kerala style. It is also famous as Kasi (Varanasi) of the South. Traditional art renditions and Elephant processions are famous here. November-December is the period of the annual festival known as Vaikathashtami. Legends cite

Parasurama's associations with the temple.

St. Mary's Church: This church in the high ranges of Karuvilangad town was built in 355 AD. The inscription on the ancient bell of the church is yet to be deciphered.

The one at Athirampuzha renovated in 1874 was built in 1080 AD. The annual feast in honour of St.Sabastian accompanied by fireworks and decorative illuminations and privileged devotees making votive offerings of gold and silver are all part of an exclusive festival here.

The 800 year old church at Kudamaloor was built by Champakasseri Maharajah. A rope and water log used to draw water from wells is the traditional offering here. The place also has a famous temple.

St. Joseph's Monastery: Situated near the Medical College at Mannanam, this church was built by the blessed Father Chavara Kuriakose Elias whose mortal remains are preserved and revered by the multitude of devotees every day.

Kaduthuruthi Valiapalli: Situated on the MC road between Ettumanoor and Vaikom, this age-old church, built in 500 AD is famous for its huge portal cross made out of a single stone.

Vimalagiri Church: This Holy place of worship stands tall as a reminder of the grandeur of Gothic architecture with its 172 ft. tower, clearly one of the tallest church towers of the State. Every December hosts a feast.

St. Thomas Church: This is again an ancient monument, built in 1002 AD and renovated in the 18th century. This is situated at Pala.

Another church, at Cherpungal, which according to a belief was built by St. Thomas and then relocated to the southern banks of the beautiful Meenachil river with the aid of poet Kunchan Nambiar and family is another age-old worship centre. The votive oblation here is oil lamps in front of the image of Infant Jesus, much similar to Hindu faith.

Aruvithira Church: 11 km off Kottayam, this church, according to a belief established by St.Thomas, is among the churches of Kerala which have a hefty inflow of pecuniary oblations during the festive occasions. A feast is celebrated in April every year.

Pazhayapalli Mosque: In Chenganacherry, 21 km off Kottayam, this famous Mosque of central Travancore was built 950 years ago. During 'Thangal Adiyanthiram', which is the famous annual festival, two tonnes of rice and hundreds of kilos of meat pour in from devotees, with which 'Biriyani' a famous cuisine of lingering taste is cooked for a grand community feast. The Mosque also celebrates another festival, the 'Chandanakudam' festival for which devotees flock in large numbers.

Thirunakkara Mahadeva Temple: Right in the heart of the city of Kottayam, this Siva temple built in the grand architectural style unique to Kerala, by the Maharajah of Tekkumkoor is half a millennium old. The walls are adorned with exquisite paintings. The 'Koothambalam', the grand edifice ad hoc to cultural congregation is one of the highlights.

Pathenpalli: In Erattupetta, this place is famous for the festival 'Chandanakudam', 'Chandan' meaning sandal and 'Kudam' meaning pot, in the months of February and December.

Saraswathi Temple: This temple, situated at Panachikkad is also known as the Southern Mookambika Temple. This temple is dedicated to Goddess Saraswathi, the Goddess for arts and learning and the consort of Lord Brahma, the creator of the Universe and everything it holds. Saraswathi Pooja is celebrated every year here in October or November. 'Vidhyarambam' is also a famous festival during which the juveniles are introduced for the first time ever in their lives to letters and other arts.

The Surya Temple: The very name of the place 'Adityapuram' which means 'Abode of Sun God' signifies the presence of the Temple dedicated to the Sun God. The first and last Sundays of the Zodiacs Scorpio which falls in the months November and December and Aries in the months of April and May are reckoned to be auspicious.

Bhagavathyamman Temple: This temple, at Ambalakadavu, dedicated to Goddess Bhagavathy is where the 'Arattu' festival of the Thirunakkara Mahadevar Temple is celebrated. The Vishu festival is also celebrated here in the months April and May.

Pallipurathukavu: This place is famous for the 'Padam Udaya Mahotsavam' and the ritual offering 'Nadel Thiyattu' performance.

Bhagavathi Temple: This temple, situated at Manarkad, dedicated to Goddess Bhadrakali was built 200 years ago. 'Kalamezhuthupattu', 'Kumbha Bharani', 'Meena Bharani', 'Patham Udayam' and 'Mandalam Chirappu' are the main festivals here.

Kavil Bhagavathy Temple: Located at Changanacherry 18 km from Kottayam, this temple dedicated to Goddess Bhagavathy, was built by the Maharajas of Thekkumkoor. 'Kavilchirappu' in December-January is the annual festival here.

Kidangoor Sri Subrahmanya Swamy Temple: The annual festival takes place between middle of March.

Sree Subramanya Swamy Temple: Sree Subramanya also known as Lord Muruga, son of the Divine couple Lord Siva and Goddess Parvathi, is the presiding deity of the Temple which is situated at Perunna, 20 km from Kottayam. The annual festival 'Pallimetta Utsavam' is celebrated here in the months of November and December.

Siva Temple and Kalkulathukavu Temple: At Vazhappalli, Changana-cherry, 17 km off Kottayam, this temple dedicated to Lord Siva abounds in ancient sculptures and ornate carvings.

The Kalkulathukavu Temple at Vazhappalli hosts a rare festival called the 'Mudiyeduppu Utsavam' which is celebrated at 12 year long intervals. Apart from other rituals the Holy procession carrying honey, known as 'Madhu' and plantain saplings and trees bearing fruits and flowers known as 'Kulavazha', 'Bhairavi Purapadu' and Darika Vadha Purappadu also form part of the grand celebrations.

Festivals

Floral Display and Victual Banquet: With the arrival of the penultimate week of the first month of the year, rapturous memories of the exuberant celebrations of the 'New Year' still lingering in the minds, various parts of the district and inundated with flowers, wild and mild with their piquant fragrance wafting through the air.

Feasts are organised as part of the annual celebrations at a number of Churches, Mosques and Temples during their respective periods.

Erumeli Petta Thullal: Erumeli, the venue of innate congenuity between Hinduism and Islamism hosts this traditional festival. The pilgrims on their way to Sabharimala halt here, offer prayers in Vavar Mosque and indulge in the legendary 'Petta

Thullal', at Sastha Temple which is, unconstrained dancing in Divine Ecstasy. This occurs in the month of January.

Vaikomashtami: This is a 12 day festival which usually falls in between November and December. Elephant processions fireworks and cultural performances like the Kathakali, Ottamthullal and musical recitals etc., are some of the highlights.

Ettumanoor Ezharapponnana: Arattu ritual, Elephant processions, procession of devotees, etc., are part of the celebrations.

Chandanakudam: The 'Chandanakudam' or 'Sandal Pot' is a 2 day festival. Cultural performances like music, dance, drama and fireworks add to the celebrations.

Ponadu Chootu Padayani: The Bhagavathy Temple at Meenachil taluk celebrates this festival annually. Devotees perform clockwise reverential circumambulation carrying lighted palm fronds and hit one another with the burning fronds as part of the ritual.

Better Home Exhibition: An exclusive fair of household articles and domestic utensils help better homes. This is held between the 2nd and the 6th October every year.

Boat Timings: The town jetty is about 1.5 km away from the KSRTC Bus Stand and during summer season the boats operates from Kodimatha Jetty is about 1 km from KSRTC Bus Terminal and 2.5 km from Railway Station.

Kottayam-Alleppey - 3 hours journey.

Kottayam-Mannar - 3 hours journey.

Kottayam-Champakulam - 4 hours journey.

District Information Offices

- District Information Officer, ©:91- 481- 2562558
- DTPC, ©:91- 481- 2560479

Accommodation

Kottayam (STD: 0481)

- **Anjali Hotel,** K.K. Road, Kottayam - 686001. ©: 2563661, 2563669.
- **Basant Hotel,** Kottayam, ©: 2561291
- **Chandravilas,** Kottayam, ©: 2568496
- **Exon Guest House** ©: 2564916
- **Highland Hotel & Resort,** X-417 A, NH-208, Kottarakara, Kollam. ©: 0474 - 2451442. Fax: + 9 1 - 0 4 7 4 - 2 4 5 5 0 6 1 . hotel@highlandindia.com
- **Hotel Aida,** M.C. Road, Kottayam-686039. Email: aida@asianetindia.com ©: 2568391. Fax: 2568399.
- **Hotel Aiswarya,** Near Thirunakkara Temple, Thirunakkara, Kottayam - 686 002.©: 2581254.
- **Hotel Anand,** Kottayam, ©: 2535586, 2560558.
- **Hotel Athira,** Kottayam, ©: 2565967

- **Hotel Floral Park,** ☎: 2597108 Fax: 2595020
- **Hotel Green Park,** Kurian Uthup Road, Nagampadom, Kottayam 686 001. Email: greenparkktm@ hotelskerala.com ☎: 2563331. Fax: 2364485.
- **Hotel Imperial,** Kottayam, ☎: 2561194
- **Hotel Kaycees Residency** ☎: 2563693
- **Hotel Kudumbam,** Kottayam, ☎: 2363211
- **Hotel Nisha Continental** ☎: 2563984
- **Hotel Nithya** ☎: 2597849/ 2590763
- **Hotel Prince** ☎: 2574483 Fax: 2573138
- **Hotel Rajaprastham,** Pattambi, Kottayam. ☎ : 0091-481-614567. Email: rajaprastham@ hotelskerala. com ☎: 2381038. Fax: 2364485.
- **Hotel Sakthi** ☎: 2563151
- **Nellimuttil Tourist Home** ☎: 2560714 Fax: 2595020
- **New Modern Hotel,** Kottayam, ☎: 2562599
- **Pride,** Kottayam, ☎: 2567348
- **The Ambassador** ☎: 2563293 Fax: 2563755
- **The Windsor Castle,** Kodimatha, Kottayam, Kerala-686039. Email: windsorktm@hotels kerala.com ☎: 2530172. Fax: 2364485
- **Tipsy Hotel** ☎: 2535541 Fax: 2536708

- **Vembanadu Lake Resort,** Kodimatha, Kottayam-686039. Email:vembanadresort@ hotelskerala.com ☎: 2381038. Fax: 2364485.
- **Vembanadu Resort** ☎: 2361633 Fax: 2360866 Email:vembanad @md5.vsnl.net.in

Kumarakom (STD: 0481)

- **Coconut Lagoon** ☎: 2525834, 2524495
- **Golden Waters** ☎: 2525826
- **Kumarakom Lake Resorts** ☎: 2524900 Fax: 2524987
- **Lakshmi Hotels,** Kavanattinkara, Kumarakom, Kottayam. ☎:2523313
- **Taj Garden Retreat,** 1/404, Kumarakom, Kottayam-686563. Email: tajretreat@hotelskerala. com ☎: 2524377.

Changanacherry (STD: 0481)

- **Breeze International Hotel,** Kavala, Changanassery, Kottayam-686101. Email: breezechngy@hotelskerala.com ☎: 2381038. Fax: 2364485.
- **Hotel Maharani,** M.C. Road, Changanassery, Kottayam-686101 Email: maharanichry@ hotelskerala.com ☎: 2428090.
- **Hotel Vani,** Central Junction, Changanassery-686101, Kottayam. Email: hotelvani@ hotelskerala. com ☎: 2427403.

Malappuram

Facts and Figures

Area : 3,548 Sq.kms.
• Population : 3,629,640 (2001 census) • Headquarters : Mallappuram • Tourist Season: September to March.

This is yet another district of Kerala with places of historic and archaeological importance. The ancient temples and mosques, the traditional system of medicine and treatment practiced here, the bird sanctuary buoyed by picturesque hillocks, the festivals and the costumes of the people, all speak volumes of the rich heritage of the district which has adopted the name of one of its major cities–Malappuram. This was incidentally the military headquarters of the popular Zamorians of Kozhikode which is about 50 kms afar.

Malappuram district is bounded by Kozhikode district on the North, The Nilgiris on the East, Arabian Sea on the West and Thrissur and Palakkad districts on the South.

Air: The nearest airport is at Karippur, Kozhikode, 36 km away.

Rail: The main railway station is at Kozhikode.

In and Around Malappuram

The Thali Temple: About 20 kms from Malappuram city is Perinthalmanna wherein this famous temple whose presiding deity is Goddess 'Durga' is situated. Angadipuram is just 3 km on the East of the place. Pooram festival is celebrated here.

Thirumandhamkunnu Temple: This temple at Angadipuram, 3 km on the west of Perinthalmanna is an important pilgrim centre, whose presiding deity is Goddess 'Durga'. In the months March and April the annual festival, Pooram is celebrated.

The Jama-at Mosque: This mosque at Malappuram attracts a large number of Muslim pilgrims from every nook and cranny of Kerala and more during the annual festival in April. The 'Mausoleum' abutting the Mosque reminisces the heroic acts of bravery of the martyrs of Malappuram - 'The Malappuram Shaheeds'.

The Pazhayangadi Mosque: This mosque is situated at Kondotti, 18 km East of Manjeri. This important pilgrim centre of the Muslims has been built 500 years ago, The annual festival unique to the place, known as the 'Valia Nercha', held in February and March is indeed a grand feast for three long days.

Tirur: (25 km West of Malappuram) The presence of the birth place of 'Thunchath Ezhuthachan', the father of the regional language of Kerala - Malayalam, is the pride of the place. The practice of acquainting toddlers with the alphabets of the fathomless Malayalam, on a small plane of sand taken from the revered spot which was once the abode of Ezhuthachan who later came to be known as Thunchan Parambu, has been going on for years together with unscathed enthusiasm.

Tanur: History suggests this coastal fishing town as one of the settlements of the Portuguese of the very early times. It is also believed that, in 1546, St. Francis Xavier visited the place.

One of the oldest temples of Kerala, 'The Keraladeshapuram Temple', dedicated to Lord Vishnu is situated about 3 km from here.

Kottakkal: The mention of the name 'Kottakkal' leads invariably to the thought of 'Arya Vaidyasala', founded by Vaidyarathnam in 1902. This pioneer institution of Ayurveda, the traditional system of health and medicine which believes in 'Prevention is better than cure' though it offers lasting cure to various diseases, has branches throughout the State and in Delhi and Chennai. Relentless in research and development the Vaidyasala runs an Ayurvedic Research Centre which also serves as a nursing home and hospital. An appointment in advance of at least 10 days is mandatory to see the chief doctor. Accommodations are available. The Ayurvedic centre is famous as P.S. Warrier, 'Kottakkal Arya Vaidyasala'.

Kottapadi: The base of the Cantonment Hill, near the health-giving Ayurvedic Centre at Kottakkal, contains cognizant evidences of an old and once magnificent fort of the Zamorins of Kozhikode. Vettakkorumakan Temple and a popular Siva Temple whose walls are adorned by the ornate paintings of Malabar are not too far away.

Kadaladi Bird Sanctuary: The sanctuary ideally studded with beautiful hillocks on a group of exhilarating islands is where the enchanting river 'Kadundipuzha' meets her destination - the Arabian Sea. It is the asylum to more than a 100 species of fascinating bird-inhabitants and 60 species of migratory birds. The awesome view of the magnificent river blending effortlessly into the mammoth sea can be had from the vantage points atop a hillock 200 m above the sea level. The place is also the fisherman's favourite as it hosts a variety of fish, mussels and crabs.

Padinjarekkara Beach: This place is where the fabulous rivers Bharathapuzha and Tirurpuzha combine and flow into the Arabian Sea. It is situated on the Tipu Sultan road near Ponnani.

The Vallikunnu Beach: A beach resort is a beauty by itself. And this beach is further beautified by the immense coconut grove that graces the place. One more spot of gleeful-awe to bird-admirers - the 'Kadaladi' Bird Sanctuary' is at a stone's throw from here.

Kadampuzha: (30 km from Malappuram) On the highway which passes by Kozhikode and Trissur, about 3 km on the North of Vettichira, the place, Kadampuzha is where the famous temple dedicated to Goddess Bagavathy, believed to have been established by Sri Adi Sankara, a great religious reformer of

Hinduism, is situated.

Trikandiyur Siva Temple: According to the legends the idol of this temple dedicated to Lord Siva, has been installed by Parasurama, the legendary creator of Kerala. It is located near Tirur.

Mamburam: It is a frequented pilgrim centre of the Muslims in A.R. Nagar Village as it is where the Mosque and Mausoleum of the religious leaders of the Malabar Muslims known locally as the 'Thangals' is situated.

Biyyan Kayal: This place near Ponnani is famous for watersports. The aquaduct amidst lush green surroundings is anyone's attraction.

Kodikuthimala: The verdant mountains with a variety of herbs and shrubs, the mighty rocks and the natural perennial springs whose cool waters calm minds are simply nature's marvel.

Tirunavai: On the banks of the river Bharathapuzha, 8 km South of Tirur, is Tirunavai, a place of historical and religious significance. In older days, the *Mamamgam* festival here was a grand assembly of rulers of Kerala, held once in 12 years. Believed to have been founded by Cheraman Perumal, it was last performed in 1755. Today, the Sarvodayamela is held in the *Navamukunda Temple* every January. This temple is said to be founded by the nine great saints and is so called the *Banares of the South*. (Open 05.00 - 11.00 hrs, 17.00 - 19.00 hrs)

Nilambur: The sylvan landscape with teeming plantations of teak and bamboo on the famous canolis plot is the original abode of one of Kerala's oldest tribes called the 'Cholanaickans'.

Visiting Hours : 10:00 - 17:00 hrs
Entrance Fee : Rs.10/-

Adyanpara: The fabulous waterfalls and the extensive woods are the natural pride of Adyanpara, located in Kurumbalangode Village of Nilambur taluk.

Festivals

Nilambur Pattu: This annual festival is celebrated with great enthusiasm in the month of February.

Neercha: This festival is held by the Mosques at Malappuram and Kondotti in the month of February and March every year. Community feast is the highlight of the celebrations.

Pooram: This is an annual Hindu festival in the months March and April. A number of faithful devotees from all over Kerala take part in the celebrations.

Tourist Information Office
• DTPC, ✆: 91-483-2731504

Accommodation

Malappuram (STD: 0483)
• Hotel Palace ✆: 2734698
• Hotel Mahendrapuri ✆: 2734102 Fax: 2734105
• Geemi Tourist Home ✆: 2734761
• Maliyakkal Tourist Home ✆: 2734513

Kottakkal (STD: 0483)
• Hotel Viraj ✆: 2743269
• Reem International ✆: 2742302
• Thayambagom Tourist Home ✆: 2743078
• Sajidha Tourist Home ✆: 2742017 Fax: 2742717

Kondotty (STD: 0483)
• Hotel Airport Plaza ✆: 2722206

Kollam

Facts and Figures

Area : 2,491 Sq.kms.
● Population : 2,584,118 (2001 census) ● Headquarters : Kollam ● Tourist Season: August to March.

This is another prodigious part of Kerala rich in ancient monuments, historic magnificent temples, rock cut caves, picnic spots and so on. The place has historical and legendary references. There are quite a few pilgrim centres where thousands of devotees congregate and perform a variety of religious rituals. It also has a unique temple at Ochira where festivals marked by not-so-usual rites take place. The remains of an ancient fort of the 18th century can also be found here.

There is a place called Thenmala which is rapidly developing into an 'Eco Tourism Spot'. This place abounds in rubber and tea plantations. The aroma of the rejuvenating tea of Kerala fills the heart of the tea-maniacs all over the world.

Kollam is connected by rail and road with several important cities and tourist centres in India. The nearest airport Thiruvanantha-puram, is 71 km away.

In and Around Kollam

Sri Maha Ganapathy Temple: Situated in Kottarakara. This temple is dedicated to both, Lord Ganapathy and His father Lord Siva. Praying to Lord Ganapathy on the commencement of every act or event is a common practice among Hindus. A festival lasting eleven days starting from the Kodiyattam is celebrated annually.

Thangasseri: This placid hamlet along the shore is one of the ancient Portuguese settlements in India. The time-worn Portuguese fort here, which stands in ruins, dates back to the 18th century. There is also a 144 ft. tall lighthouse which can be visited between 15.30 and 17.30 hrs. The town buses ply between Kollam and here every 15 mts.

Mayyanad: About 10 km South of Kollam, Mayyanad is a Holy land of Temples as there are as many as 9 of them. The Subramanya Swamy Temple at Umayanallur dedicated to the Lord Subramanya or Muruga has, according to the legends, been consecrated by the great religious and social reformer Sri Adi Sankara. There are busses in quick succession from Kollam to Mayyanad.

Sasthankotta: This is an important pilgrim spot, 29 km from Kollam, where the ancient Sastha Temple dedicated to the Lord 'Ayyappa' is situated. It is evident that the name of the town owes its origin to the temple. The place also has a wide fresh water lake, a captivating one with elegant hills aptly located on all the three sides to make every onlooker get carried away. Busses frequent between here and Kollam. P.W.D. offers accommodation at the rest house.

Ochira: It is here, 34 km North of Kollam Town that the unique 'Parabrahma Temple' is situated. The temple has no idol, no deity and is dedicated to the 'Universal Consciousness' instead. This Pilgrim Center is no less famous than any other. The Ochira Kali and the 'Panthrandu Vilakku' are the two main festivals celebrated here, the former in the middle of June and the latter in the months November and December. As part of the Ochira Kali celebrations, men form groups donning warriors attires of the historic era and enact a mock fight between themselves on the spot 'Padanilam' which means battlefield. Another strange performance is the martial dance by devotees in knee-deep water wielding their swords and flashing their shields, splashing the water all over in the process. The 'Panthrandu Vilakku' which means twelve lamps is a festival which lasts for 12 days. The place has busses frequently to Kollam and Alapuzha.

Kulathupuzha: Situated on the Senkottai-Thiruvananthapuram Road, 64 km off Kollam, this place has a temple dedicated to Lord Ayyappa or Sastha, known as the 'Sastha Temple'. The important festival here is the 'Vishu Mahotsavam' which is celebrated in April and May every year. Frequent busses are available to Kollam and Alapuzha. The nearest railway station, 'Thenmala' is about 10 km away.

Thenmala: This region has a plenty of rubber and tea plantations. The tea of the region is much sought after while the rubber has an equal appeal. Efforts are on to develop the place into a spot of 'Eco Tourism'. It has a leisure zone that includes winding pathways, a sway bridge, a sculpture garden and a boardwalk. Other attractions are the Deer Rehabilitation Centre and the adjacent shenduruney wildlife sanctuary. There is also a dam here.

Ariankavu: This is again a famous pilgrim spot of the Hindus with a Temple dedicated to the Lord 'Ayyappa' also known as Sri Sastha. Mandala Pooja and Trikalyanam are the two major festivals here. Busses from Kollam to Ariankavu, on way to Senkottai, covering a distance of 70 km are frequent.

Palaruvi Waterfalls: Located at about 75 km from Kollam, 'Palaruvi' which as a matter of fact means 'Milkfalls' is an excellent picnic spot. Scores of picnic makers are lured by the charms of the waters making an abrupt fall from a height of 300 ft. as if relieved from the tedious roll down the robust rocks. The surrounding jungle adds to the grandeur of the area. Accommodations are available at the P.W.D. inspection bungalow and the KTDC Motel.

Matha Amrithanandamayi Ashram: The Ashram of Matha Amrithanandamayi situated at

Amrithapuri near Vallikavu is also the headquarters of the Matha's Ashrams. The ashram can be reached by boat; however, there is also a road link.

Thirumullavaram Beach: This beach in recluse as if in search of solitude, is a placid picnic spot. The palm trees around add to the calm that surrounds. Frequent busses help visitors get to the spot from the town.

Picnic Village: Recreation is at a high in the Picnic Village located at Ashramam in Kollam. The back water here is typical of the Kerala backwaters. A Government guest house built two centuries ago, a tourist boat club, an adventure park, a traffic park for children imparting the important knowledge of traffic rules and their importance in the young all-grasping minds and a 'Yathri Nivas' are among the salient features.

Kottukkal Rock Cut Cave Temple: Separated from Chadayamangalam, by a mere 11 km on the M.C. Road between Thiruvananthapuram and Kottayam, this temple is an excellent specimen of rock cut architecture. Hundreds of visitors, come, stand and admire.

Jatayu Para: This is a huge rock at Chadayamangalam on which, as the legend says, the Mythical Eagle 'Jatayu' breathed His last after His bid to avert the demon King Ravana abducting Sita, Rama's spouse, went in vain. 'Jatayu' as was called the mythical Eagle and 'Para', meaning rock constitute the name of the gigantic rock of mythical importance.

Backwater tours: ATDC and DTPC operate Kollam-Alapuzha boat cruises (Departure: 10:30 hrs from the boat jetty) **Fare:** Rs.300 per person.

Half way journey from Kollam to Alumkadavu: Rs. 150 per person. Concession offered to International Student Card holders.

DTPC backwater village cruise on country boat (09:00 - 13:30 hrs, 14:00 - 18:30 hrs). **Fare:** Rs.300 per person.

DTPC House boat tariff ranges from Rs.3500/- to 7500/- for 2 persons for 24 hours.

Houseboat Operators: Tour India, Thiruvananthapuram. Ph. : 0471-2331507 DTPC, Kollam Ph. : 2742558 Fax: 2742558. Email: dtpcqIn@md3. vsnl.net.in

Soma Houseboats, Thiruvananthapuram Ph. : 0471-2268101 ATDC Ph. : 0477-2243462

Exclusive Houseboat Holiday Packages from DTPC - Kollam.

Exotic blue water houseboat cruises:

Round trip cruise: Departure: 11:00 hrs from Kollam. Arrival: 17:00 hrs at Kollam. **Tariff:** Single bedroom: Rs.3000. Double bedroom: Rs.4000.

See & Sleep cruise (Day cruise with overnight stay in the houseboat): Departure: 14:00 hrs. from Kollam. Overnight stay: 18:00-06:00 hrs. Arrival at Kollam (2nd day):08:00 hrs. **Tariff:** Single bedroom: Rs.3000, Double bedroom: Rs.4000.

Star night cruise (Sunset cruise & night stay on the backwater): Departure: 17:00 hrs. from Kollam. Overnight stay: 18:30-06:30 hrs. Arrival at Kollam (2nd day): 07:30 hrs. **Tariff:** Single bedroom: Rs.2000 Double bedroom: Rs.3500.

Houseboat Cruise & Resort Stay Package

Full day cruise in Kollam DTPC's Houseboat and stay in a reputed backwater resort.

Majestic cruise: Departure: 10:00 hrs. from Kollam. Arrival: 17:00 hrs. at Ashtamudi Backwater Resort with A/c suite room. Departure from Ashtamudi Resort: 08:00 hrs. Arrival at Kollam (2nd day):09.30 hrs. **Tariff (all inclusive):** Single family: Rs.5500. Double family: Rs.9000.

Elegant cruise & resort stay: 10:00 hrs. from Kollam Arrival: 17:00 hrs. at Palm Lagoon Backwater Resort, with natural cottage accommodation and special seafood cuisine. Departure:08:00 hrs. from Palm Lagoon Resort. Arrival at Kollam (2nd day): 09:30 hrs. **Tariff (all inclusive):** Single family: Rs.3000, Double family: Rs.6000.

Houseboat cruise with Kathakali performance package

Full day houseboat cruise, Kathakali performance in the Sunset hours and night stay on board the houseboat. Departure: 13:00 hrs. from Kollam. Performance of Kathakali at Thouryathrika performing art

centre: 16:00-18:30 hrs. Overnight stay: 18:30 - 06:30 hrs. Arrival at Kollam (2nd day): 10:00 hrs.

Tariff (all inclusive): Single bedroom: Rs.5500, Double bedroom: Rs.7000.

Royal gateway city packages

Covers all backwater towns in Kerala - Kollam, Alappuzha, Kumarakom, Kottayam and Kochi. Tariff inclusive of hire, food and bata.

Kollam - Alumkadavu - Kollam & Kollam - Amrithapuri - Kollam: Full day cruise (If trip starts at 10:00 hrs from Kollam, the boat will be back at Kollam by 18:00 hrs.). **Tariff:** Single - Rs.3750, Double - Rs.4350, Conference Hall - Rs.3500.

Kollam-Kayamkulam- Kollam: Full day cruise and night stay (If trip starts at 10:00 hrs. from Kollam it will be back at Kollam by 10:00 hrs. the next morning). **Tariff:** Single - Rs.6500, Double - Rs. 8200.

Kollam-Alappuzha (one way): Full day cruise and night stay (If trip starts at 10:00 hrs. from Kollam, it will reach at Alappuzha by 10:00 hrs. next morning). **Tariff:** Single - Rs.8175, Double - Rs.10,125.

Kollam-Alappuzha-Kumarakom/Kottayam: Two days and one night stay (If trip starts at 10:00 hrs. from Kollam, it will reach Kumarakom/Kottayam on the 2nd afternoon). **Tariff:** Single - Rs.12,300, Double - Rs.14,420.

Kollam-Alappuzha-Kochi: Two days and two nights (If the trip starts at 10:00 hrs. from Kollam, it will reach Kochi on the third morning at 10:00 hrs.). **Tariff:** Single - Rs.16,350, Double - Rs.17,750.

Additional day Single - Rs.500 per hour. Additional night stay (12 hours) Single - Rs.1500.

Note: Tourists can decide the departure and arrival points (Alumkadavu to Alappuzha, Alappuzha to Amrithapuri Ashram, Kollam to Alappuzha, Kochi to Kollam, Kumarakom to Kollam, etc.). Tariff subject to changes according to destination opted.

Kollam-Alappuzha/Alappuzha-Kollam cruises

The internationally popular regular one way - 8 hour - backwater cruise between Kollam and Alappuzha/Alappuzha - Kollam is specially designed on a doubledeck cruiser. Departure: 10:00 hrs. from Kollam. Arrival: 18:00 hrs. at Alappuzha. **Tariff:** Adult (per person): Full way Rs.150, Half way - Rs.100.

Children (below 12 years): Full way Rs.100, Half way Rs.100. International Student Card Holders: Full way Rs.100, Half way Rs.100.

Canal Cruises

Kayalpradakshin Backwater Village Tour: Kollam DTPC's prestigious canal cruises to the Munroe island village is the best of its kind in India. Departure:

09:00 hrs. from Kollam. Arrival: 13:00 hrs. at Kollam. **Fare:** Adult: Rs.300 per person Children (below 12 years) : Free.

Tourist boat cruises: The mechanised and motorised tour section of DTPC has a wide range of luxury boats for backwater cruises on the Ashtamudi Backwaters.

Type of boat, capacity & fare

Ashtamudi (luxury cruiser): 150 pax capacity: Rs.1000/hr. Rs.7000 for 8 hours.

Ms. Vatsala (luxury boat): 60 pax capacity: Rs.500/hr. Rs.3500 for 8 hours.

Yatrika (open safari boat): 10 pax capacity: Rs.200/hr. Rs.1400 for 8 hours.

Aranya (closed safari boat): 8 pax capacity: Rs.300/hr. Rs.2100 for 8 hours.

Pedal/Row boats: 4 persons/ 2 persons capacity: Rs.20/person/hr.

Ethnic tours

Kairali darshan: DTPC's ethnic tour of the art, culture and traditions of interior Kerala by luxury coach.(Departure: 08:00 hrs. Arrival: 19:00 hrs.). **Fare:** Rs.750 per person.

For more details, please contact: The Administrative Office, District Tourism Promotion Council, Govt.Guest House Complex, Ashramam, Kollam. Ph : 2750170 Email:dtpcqln@md3.vsnl.net.in.

Tourist Reception Centre (DTPC), KSRTC Bus Stand, Kollam. Ph. : 2745625

Tourist Information Centre (DTPC), Railway Station, Platform No.4, Kollam.

Festivals

Ochira Kali: This is a festival unique to the place, celebrated in the middle of June every year.

Panthrandu Vilaku: This is a 12 day festival celebrated in November/December.

Vishu Mahotsavam: It occurs in the months of April/May and a number of devotees eagerly take part.

Crafts Festival: It is high time craftsmen made merry. This festival is widely celebrated featuring the conscientious work of the craftsmen. It falls in between December/January.

Tourist Information Offices

* **DTPC Tourist Information Centre,** KSRTC Bus Stand, ✆: 91-474-2745625
* **DTPC Tourist Office,** Guest House Complex, Asramam. ✆: 91-474-2750170

* **Department of Tourism - District Office,** Govt. Guest House . ✆: 91-471-2743620

Accommodation

Kollam (STD: 0474)

* **Aquaserene** ✆: 2512410 Fax: 2512104 **Email**:aquaserene.@md3.vsnl.net.in
* **Palm Lagoon** ✆: 2548974 Fax: 2548974 **Email**:palmlagoon@spectrum.net.in
* **Prasanthi Hotels (Quilon) Pvt. Ltd.** ✆: 2742292 Fax: 2742792
* **Sha International** ✆: 2742362 Fax: 2726055
* **Lake View** ✆: 2701546 **Email**:valiyavila@rediffmail.com
* **Sea Bee** ✆:2744696 Fax: 2744158
* **Hotel Sudarshan** ✆: 2744322 Fax: 2740480 **Email**:comfort@md4.vsnl.net.in

Paying Guest Accommodation

* Prof. K.R.C Nair, Ambadi Lake Resorts, Asramam, Kollam. (Approved by Dept. of Tourism) ✆:2744688

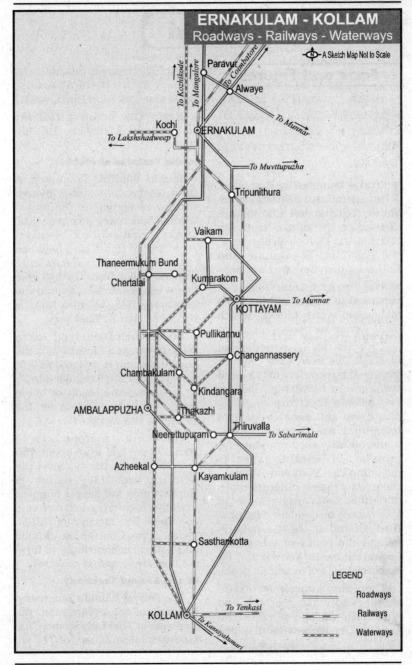

Idukki

Facts and Figures

Area : 5,019 Sq.kms.
● Population : 1,128,605 (2001 census) ● Headquarters : Painavu ● Tourist Season: August to March.

Idukki is bounded by Kottayam, Pathanamthitta districts on the South, Trichur and Coimbatore district on the north, Madurai, Ramnad and Tirunelveli district on the east and Ernakulam and Kottayam districts on the west.

The district's name 'Idukki' is supposed to be derived from the Malayalam word 'Idukku' which means a narrow gauge.

This district is a medley of marvels. The wavy ghat regions, inhabited by a variety of flora and fauna are of bewitching beauty. The wildlife sanctuary spanning over a vast area near a huge dam forming a weir between hills, benevolently accommodates a number of wildlife species including the 'National Animal', the mighty tigers, different types of reptiles and a large number of fascinating birds. The 'National Bird' of India, the peacock is among the peaks of attraction. Earavikulam is known for its pedigree breed of mountain goats.

There are summer resorts of subtle beauty and cascades and waterfalls adding glitz to the glamour. The highest South Indian peak Anamalai is situated here.

Air: The nearest international airport is at Nedumbassery, Ernakulam, 107 km North west.

Rail: The nearest railway station is at Kottayam, 133 km away.

In the Vastness of Idukki

Idukki Wildlife Sanctuary: A game reserve comparable, though smaller to Periyar is the idukki Wildlife Sanctuary, just above the Idukki Arch dam. This comprises 70 sq.km. of forest land between the *Periyar* and *Cheruthoni,* situated 40 km. from Thodupuzha. There is a scenic lake around the sanctuary. The wildlife here is similar to that at Thekkady.

Idukki Arch Dam: Built across the Kuravan and Kurathi hills the huge dam, 550 ft. tall and 650 ft. wide, facilitating a regular supply of water has the credit of being the first arch dam of Asia and the second of the world.

Gracing a generous area of about 77 sq. km, from about 450 to 748 m above the sea level the wildlife sanctuary which is situated near the dam is home to a number of common and rare land creatures and fascinating birds. Three dams, Cheruthoni, Idukki and Kulamavu contribute to form a 33 sq. km. expanse of water.

In and Around Thekkady

The Periyar Wildlife Sanctuary: Redolent of spice plantation, the resplendent Thekkady is where the far-reaching sanctuary of 777 sq.

km. is situated. The sanctuary having lent a sizable slice of about 360 sq. km. of its coveted landscape to a verdant, thick evergreen forest has to its credit a great number of wild lives. It was also declared a 'Tiger Reserve' in the year 1978. The grounds here flash with pride more than 1965 species of flowering plants, 143 species of orchids and 171 species of grass. Among the roaming wild-life are Wild Elephants, Gaur, Sambar Deer, Wild boar, etc., which make up to over 35 species.

The beautiful artificial lake formed by the Mullai Periyar Dam built across the Periyar river provides a spellbinding view of the nonchalantly captivating creatures of the wild, from a boat, close and yet safe. This 'Never-before' experience enthralls tourists from various parts of the Nation as much as those from overseas.

Visiting Hours: 06:00 - 18:00 hrs.

Kumily: About 4 km from Thekkady, on the outskirts of the Periyar Sanctuary, this place is known much as a plantation town, thanks to the fertility of its vast landscape. It is also a sought-after shopping centre and obviously spice trade is rampant. This is also the bus terminal for the Periyar region and accommodations are available here.

Murikkady: Situated 5 km from Thekkady, this place abounds in spice and coffee plantations. The spices have a good appeal and the flavour of the coffee of the place reaches far and wide.

Pandikuzhi: About 5 km from Kumily, this place has an assortment of eye pleasing flowers

and a good lot of animals. The splashing streams of smashing beauty add to the splendour. It is near the Tamil Nadu border.

Mangala Devi Temple: Encapsuled in thick forests this ancient temple atop a peak, 1337m above the sea level is a revelation of the traditional style of the grand architecture of Kerala. It is situated about 15 km from Thekkady. The access to the temple remains cut off on all other days than the day of Chithra Pournami Festival, when there is a heavy rush of devotees.

The peak also offers a scintillating view of the inclines of the eastern ghats and hamlets of the contiguous State 'Tamil Nadu'. A visit to the temple requires permission from wildlife warden, Thekkady who can be contacted over phone : 2322027.

Chellarkovil: This placid village, 15 km from Kumily, has the riches of beautiful plains and water cascades. The slopes of this village hills lead to the famous coconut groves of cumbum in Tamil Nadu, the neighbouring State.

Vandiperiyar: This is a popular place of plantations, 18 km from Thekkady. The periyar river courses along beautifully through the centre of the town facilitating a high yield from the tea, coffee and pepper plantations of the region. The place, in which a number of tea factories thrive, is obviously an important trade centre. Rows of sparklingly beautiful beautiful rose, exciting orchids and anthuria are displayed in the government agricultural farm here.

Vandanmedu: The name Vandanmedu is familiar among the cardamom traders as it is one of the world's largest auction centres. The place is surfeited with cardamom plantations whose enchanting fragrance greets every bypasser. It is 25 km from Kumily.

Pullumedu: This stupendous hill town with the nourishment of the Periyar river is about 43 km from Thekkady. Typical of a ghat

section, the region blanketed by rich greenery, punctuated with scenic hills welcomes the visitors with its exotic range of flora and fauna and natural meadows and lawns. The famous pilgrim spot, Sree Ayyappa Temple at Sabharimala where thousands of devotees throng and the Makara

Jothi illuminations are sights to revere from here. Visitors to the place are required to obtain permission from the Wildlife Preservation Officer, Thekkady whose phone number is 2322027 or the Range Officer at Vallakadhavu on the number 2352515.

Peermedu: Peermedu is a small hill station on the way to Thekkady. It is a fertile land at an altitude of 914 metres. This tiny and cool hill station is full of *rubber, tea, coffee, pepper and cardamom* plantations, intersquessed with waterfalls and open grass lands.

Ramakalmedu: 16 km from Nedumkandam, Thekkady-Munnar Road. Rolling green hills and the fresh mountain air make Ramakalmedu an enchanting

retreat. The hilltop also offers a panoramic view of the picturesque villages of Bodi and Cumbum on the eastern slope of the Western Ghats. Distance 45 km from Idukki, 40 km from Thekkady and 75 km from Munnar. Bus timings: 09.30 a.m. Munnar, 10.30 a.m. Kottayam, 09.30 a.m. Ernakulam.

In and Around Peermedu

Kuttikanam: This is the place for adventurers and trekkers, and also those who love to be lost in

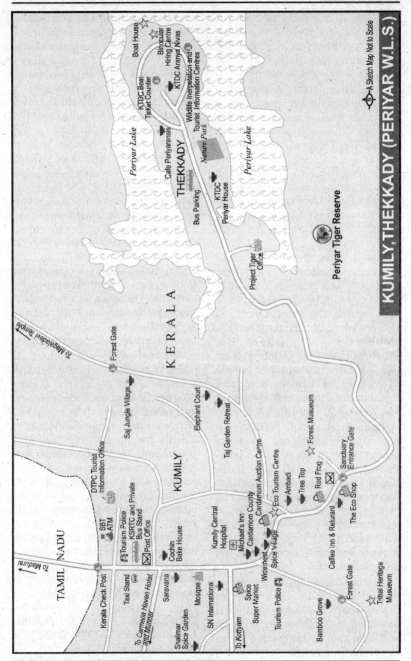

KUMILY, THEKKADY (PERIYAR W.L.S.)

A Sketch Map Not to Scale

Boat House
Binocular
Hiring Centre
KTDC Aranya Nivas
KTDC Boat
Ticket Counter
Wildlife Interpretation and
Tourist Information Centres
Cafe Periyarensis
THEKKADY
Periyar Lake
Nature Park
Periyar Lake
Bus Parking
KTDC
Periyar House
Periyar Tiger Reserve
Project Tiger
Office
KERALA
Forest Gate
To Mangaladevi Temple
Saj Jungle Village
Elephant Court
Taj Garden Retreat
Forest Museum
KUMILY
Cardamom Auction Centre
Eco Tourism Centre
Ambadi
Tree Top
Red Frog
Sanctuary
Entrance Gate
DTPC Tourist
Information Office
KSRTC and Private
Bus Stand
Post Office
Cardamom County
Michael's Inn
Kumily Central
Hospital
Cochin
Bake House
SBT
ATM
Tourism Police
The Eco Shop
Caffee Inn & Returant
Forest Gate
Widernest
Spice Village
Tourism Police
Spice
Super Market
Mosque
SN International
Saravana
Shalimar
Spice Garden
Taxi Stand
Kerala Check Post
TAMIL NADU
To Madurai
To Carmelia Haven Hotel,
and Munnar
To Kottyam
Bamboo Grove
Tribal Heritage
Museum

the serene solitude of natural splendour. It is green everywhere on the picturesque hills and the cardamom plantations fill the air with their sweet scent.

Thrissanku Hills: About 4 km from Peermede and just half a kilometer from Kuttikanam is yet another astounding part of the Earth, 'The Thrissanku Hills'. The gregarious hills with a generous green coating and strong wind intercepted by the intriguing hills to form a mild breeze is an ideal spot to watch the Sunrise and the Sunset. A stroll through the place is rejuvenating.

Peeru Hills: Just 1 km from Kuttikanam and about 4 km from Peermedu this place is named in memory of an Islamic Saint, Peer Mohammed. The Saint is believed to have spent his last days on this wonderful place where His Mausoleum can also be found. Near the place are the summer palace of the royal family and the residence of Diwan. Picnic-makers and trekkers frequent this place.

Grampi: Grampi, otherwise known as 'Parunthupara', meaning 'Eagle Rock' is about 5 km from Peermede and 10 km from Vandiperiyar. The high peaks here renders a panoramic view of the remarkable landscape lying below and hence the name 'Eagle Rock'. The road to Grampi passes by extensive plantations of coffee, tea and cardamom.

Pattumala: About 17 km on the east of Peermedu and 28 km on the west of Thekkady, Pattumala, meaning 'Silk Mountain' with its soft and gentle landscape is an entertaining region of soaring peaks and beautiful little streams. This is a place of proliferating tea plantations. The Velankanni Matha Church, built out of granite stone, makes it a popular pilgrim centre. The flower garden nearby with its flashy colours and placid flowers, ornate orchids and anthurium is an irresistable invitation to the tourist.

Vegamon: 25 km from Peermede, the grassy hills, wide open lawns and a beautiful landscape, all constitute the splendid picnic spot vegamon. There is also a chain of three distinct hills (viz) 'The Thangal Hill', 'The Murugan Hill', and 'The Karisumala', which is considered to be a natural symbol of religious harmony. There is also a dairy farm managed by monks. This place is a confluence of religious mysticism and European legacies.

Sahyadri Ayurvedic Centre: A place that holds promise for the dismayed, the Ayurvedic Centre offers treatment packages for cure and rehabilitation. It is equipped with excellent facilities including a unit for manufacturing and processing Ayurvedic medicines. A herb museum houses over 200 varieties of rare herbs of high medicinal value as part of an attempt to perpetuate the precious herbs pushed to the verge of extinction. Over 400 herb varieties are grown here in a garden of about 35 acres in area. The garden, which belongs to the hospital, can be visited with the permission of the Director, Peermedu Development Society, Peermedu, Idukki, Ph. : 2332097 & 2332247, Fax: 2332096.

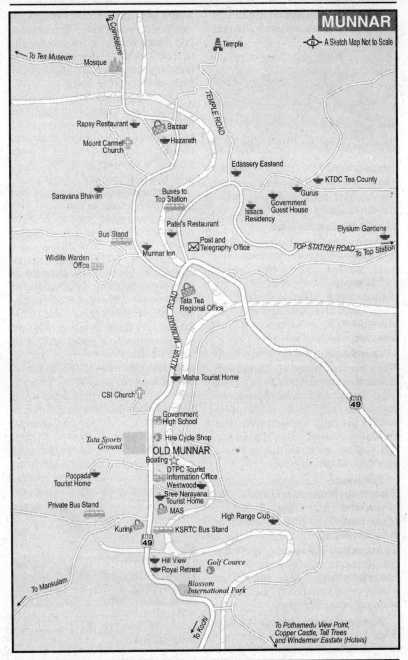

MUNNAR

A Sketch Map Not to Scale

To Tea Museum

Mosque

To Coimbatore

Temple

Rapsy Restaurant
Bazaar
Hazarath
Mount Carmel Church

TEMPLE ROAD

Edassery Eastend

KTDC Tea County

Saravana Bhavan

Buses to Top Station

Gurus
Government Guest House

Issacs Residency

Patel's Restaurant

Bus Stand

Elysium Gardens

Munnar Inn

Post and Telegraphy Office

TOP STATION ROAD
To Top Station

Wildlife Warden Office

ALUVA - MUNNAR ROAD

Tata Tea Regional Office

Misha Tourist Home

CSI Church

49

Tata Sports Ground

Government High School

Hire Cycle Shop

OLD MUNNAR

Boating

Poopada Tourist Home

DTPC Tourist Information Office
Westwood
Sree Narayana Tourist Home
MAS

Private Bus Stand

High Range Club

Kurinji

KSRTC Bus Stand

49

To Mankulam

Hill View
Royal Retreat

Golf Cource

Blossom International Park

To Kochi

To Pothamedu View Point, Copper Castle, Tall Trees and Windermer Eastate (Hotels)

Munnar - Hill Station: It is 129 kms from Cochin, with an altitude

ranging from 1600 to 1800 metres above sea level. Munnar boasts of the highest peak in South India. *Anamudi* 2695 metres high.

In and Around Munnar

Pothanmedu: Pothanmedu, possesses enormous plantations of tea, coffee and the spice cardamom. Pervaded by picturesque hills and verdant mountains, the place attracts a lot of trekkers. It can be reached from Munnar which is just 6 km away.

Devikulam: About 7 km from Munnar, this place has a natural mineral water lake known as the 'Sita Devi Lake' which lends its name to the place. Devikulam which literally means that 'the Pond of Goddess'. This is a serene hill station with all the richness of a typical ghat region.

Pallivasal: This place is situated 8 km from Munnar and is the site of the first Hydro Electric Project of the State. The place abounds in natural beauty.

Attukkal: This place, just 9 km off Munnar, is famous for its waterfalls and serene hills. This place is situated in between Munnar and Pallivasal.

Nyayamakad: About 10 km from Munnar, between Rajamala and Munnar, this naturally gifted

place has all the beauties of an awesome waterfalls. The waters roll down the hills from a height of 1600 m in a splendid cascade gaining momentum with every inch of their long track.

Chithirapuram: Separated from Munnar by 10 km, this spot has beautiful little cottages, grand bungalows, old playgrounds and courts. Pallivasal Hydel Power Project is located here. There are also tea plantations.

Mattupetty: This is a wonderful place with a lake and a dam. The sheet of water squired by mighty mountains make it a fine picnic spot. There are also tea plantations, DTPC Idukki offers boating facilities. The altitude of the region is about 1700 m above sea level. There is a highly specialised dairy farm - the Indo-Swiss Livestock Project. Visitors are permitted to enter only 3 of the 11 cattlesheds here.

Boat Rentals : 09:30-15:00 hrs.
Speed launch: Rs.300 for 15 min.
(max 5 persons)
Safari boat : Rs.700 for 30 min.
(for 25 persons)
Visiting Hours : 9:00-11:00 hrs.
Entrance Fee : Rs.5/- per head

Echo Point: About 15 km from Munnar, this is the place where, as the name suggests, the natural

echo phenomenon takes place. It is on the way to the top station from Munnar.

Eravikulam National Park: This park spans over an area of 97 sq. km in the Devikulam Taluk about 15 km from Munnar. This place again, abounds in flora and fauna. Among the exotic fauna of here are the Nilgiri Tahr and a pedigree breed of cattle. The Anamudi Peak, 2695m above the sea level is situated here.

Visiting Hours : 08:00 - 17:00 hrs
Entrance Fee : Rs.10/- for Adults, Rs.2/- for children below 12 years and Rs.50/- for foreigners

Rajamalai: Among the original inhabitant variety of animal species of the region is the 'Nilgiri Tahr' whose population is dwindling. The total number of

them according to an estimate, is a mere 1317 (subject to variations in number with time). The Rajamalai region is the only region out of the three in the park, in which tourists are allowed, the other two being the buffer and the core area.

Visiting Hours : 7:00-18:00 hrs. (Entry prohibited during monsoon)
Entrance Fee : Rs.10/- for Adults, Rs.5/- for children below 12 years and Rs.50/- for foreigners

Power House Waterfalls: 18 km from Munnar, this place is worth a halt on the way to the Periyar wildlife sanctuary. The inspiring cascade of the enormous waters down the steep rock 2000 m above the sea level is there to stand and admire. The scenery of the gregarious western mountains leave in the minds a lasting impression.

Kundala: 20 km from Munnar the beautiful town of Kundala is situated on the way to the top station. The vast Golf course located here belongs to Tata Tea Ltd. The presence of Kundala dam adds to the charm. The wonderful waterfall of 'Aruvikkad' is located near 'Kundala'.

Anayirankal: This wonderful place is about 22 km from Munnar. The delightful dam and the beautiful reservoir amidst a vast expanse of aromatic tea plantations of the Tata Tea Ltd. and the evergreen forests all combine to make it an ideal picnic spot.

Top Station: As it is rightly called, the 'Top Station', it is the highest point in Munnar, about 1700 m above sea level, on the Munnar-Kodaikanal Road, about 32 km from Munnar. The exotic flower 'Neelakurinji' is said to hail from this region. These flowers appear in brilliant blue but only once in 12 long years and when they do, the entire region gets smeared by the rare but sure beauty. An areal view of parts of the adjoining State Tamil Nadu can also be had from here.

Marayoor: The mention of the name Marayoor which is 40 km off Munnar sends the scent of sandal in the air. This is the only place in Kerala where there is a natural growth of Sandalwood Trees. The place cherishes the subtle fragrance. The Forest Department runs a sandalwood factory. There are also wonderful caves whose walls are adorned with painting and sculptures relating to the 'New Stoneage Civilization'. The children's park and a huge banyan tree are among the salient features. Thoovanam waterfalls and the Rajiv Gandhi National park are close by.

Cheeyapara: The marvellous waterfalls of Cheeyapara is simply a visual feast as the waters roll down in a seven step cascade. Cheeyapara and Valara waterfalls are located between Neriamangalam and Adimali on the Kochi-Madurai highway. This place also attracts trekkers.

Meenuli: A mammoth rock of about 500 acres in area upon which spreads two lavish acres of beautiful evergreen forest is behind the fame of the place which challenges mountaineers.

Malankara Reservoir: 6 km from Thodapuzha, this is a wonderful artificial lake. Boating and fishing are very popular here.

Thommankuthu: About 28 km from Thodapuzha, the waterfalls here again like the 'Cheeyapara falls' flow down a flight of seven steps in a captivating cascade forming a pool beneath each step. Adventurers are attracted to the place in large numbers.

Kalvari Mount: This is a famous pilgrim centre on the way to Kattappana.

Chinnar Wildlife Sanctuary: About 60 km from Munnar, on the Kerala-Tamil Nadu border, this sanctuary spreading over 90.44 sq. km. is an asylum to a number of animal and bird species.

Visiting Hours : 7:00-18:00 hrs A visit to the sanctuary requires the permission of the Wildlife Warden, Idukki Wild Division, Painau/Wildlife DFO, Munnar, Ph.: 2530487.

TEMPLES AND FESTIVALS

Sree Krishna Temple: This temple is dedicated to Lord Krishna. It is located at Peermedu, 42 km from Kumili.

The ten day annual festival ceremoniously commences with the hoisting of the temple flag (Kodiyettam). The last two evenings are marked by lively performances of *'Ottanthullal', Kavadiyattam.*

On the last night, the *'Thidampu'* is taken out for the *'Arattu'* (holy bath). This colourful procession, with the Thidampu ceremoniously carried on a caparisoned elephant to the accompaniment of the temple music, *Panchavadyam',* marks the conclusion of the festival.

Sree Dharmasastha Temple, Vazhathoppu, Idukki: This temple is dedicated to Lord Dharmasastha (Ayyappa, son of Shiva and Vishnu in the female form of Mohini - the temptress). The annual one day colourful festival is celebrated in pomp and splendour. *'Ammankudam'* and *'Thalappoli', 'Garudanvaravu'* (a folk ritual) representing the celestial bird, Garuda (the vehicle of Vishnu) is also performed during the festival.

Sree Murugan Kovil, Munnar: This temple is dedicated to *Lord Subrahmanya,* also known as Sree Muruga - son of Lord Siva. The one day festival is known as *'Thrikkarthika Utsavam'.*

Sree Ayyappa Temple, Anachal, Munnar: This temple is dedicated to Lord Ayyappa. It is situated at Anachal, 15 km from Munnar. The six day annual festival commences with the ceremonial hoisting of the temple flag (Kodiyettam).

Santhigiri Sree Maheswari Temple, Adimali: This temple dedicated to Lord Siva is situated at Santhigiri at the heart of Adimali town. It celebrates a five day festival every year. The last day *'Sivarathri'* is considered most auspicious for worship.

Sree Parthasarathy Temple, Mundakkayam: This temple at Mundakkayam, 65 km from Thekkady, is dedicated to Lord Parthasarathy. The six day festival commences with the ceremonial hoisting of the temple flag (Kodiyettam).

Sree Krishnaswamy Temple: Thodupuzha: The temple, dedicated to Lord Krishna, is located at the heart of Thodupuzha town. It celebrates a ten day festival every year. *'Kathakali'* performances are also held on 5th and 6th days.

For Tourists' Information

A number of facilities as the local transport, communication, banks & currency exchanges, Ayurveda hospitals and Allopathic hospitals are available both in Thekkady and Munnar.

The Kerala Tourism Development Corporation (K.T.D.C.) along with other departments like the Forest Department offer a well organised network of package tours to cater to the needs of various tourists. Information about the accommodation, mountaineering, boating etc., can be obtained from the respective departments. In an attempt to facilitate the tourist, we have provided the telephone numbers then and there. And given below are two important numbers which would serve as a ready-reckoner.

The Forest Department: 2322028
KTDC : 2322023

BOAT CRUISES

The forest department and the KTDC conduct boating trips from Periyar Lake, Thekkady.

Entrance fee at check-post: Foreigners: Rs.50/- (valid for 3 days) and Domestic Tourists: Rs.2/-.

For advance booking contact: KTDC, Ph: 2322023 and Forest Department, Ph: 2322028.

Tourist Information Offices

• **District Tourist Information Office,** Department of Tourism, Thekkady Jn.,Kumily ✆ : 9 1 - 4869-222620

• **DTPC Information Centre,** Munnar. Telefax:91-4865-231516 Email:info@dtpcidukki.com

Accommodation

Thekkady (STD: 04869)

• **Taj Garden Retreat (4 Star)** ✆: 222401-08 Fax: 222106 **Email**:retreat.thekkady@ tajhotels.com

- **Aranya Nivas (KTDC) (3 Star)**
  ✆: 222023 Fax: 222282
  Email:aranyanivas@vsnl.com
- **Lake Palace (KTDC)** ✆: 222024
  Fax:222282 Email:ktdc@vsnl.com
- **Spice Village** ✆: 222314-16 Fax:
  222317
- **Cardamom County** ✆: 222806
  Fax: 222807 Email:cardamom
  county@vsnl.com
- **Periyar House (KTDC)**
  ✆: 222447 Fax: 222526
- **Leela Pankaj** ✆: 222392 Fax:
  222392

Peermedu (STD: 04869)

- **Thrissanku Haven, Kuttikanam**
  ✆: 222491 Fax: 232692
  Email:trisangu@md4.vsnl.net.in
- **Misty Mountain, Kuttikanam**
  ✆: 232065

Munnar (STD: 04865)

- **Abad Copper Castle Resort**
  ✆: 230633/230443 Fax: 230438
- **Status Resorts (Cottages)**
  ✆: 230688 Fax: 230538
- **Mahindra Resorts** ✆: 249292
  Fax: 04868-249227 Email:
  anilkumar@mahindraholidays.com
- **Sterling Resorts** ✆: 249207 Fax:
  04868 - 249206
- **Periyar Mist Valley** ✆: 230708
  Fax: (0484) 238664
- **Mist Valley Resort (Cottages)**
  ✆: 230708
- **High Range Club** ✆: 230724 Fax:
  230333
- **Copper Castle** ✆: 230633 Fax:
  230438
- **Tea County** ✆: 230460
  Fax: 230970 Email:
  teacountymunnar@ ktdc.com
- **Star Homes Igloo** ✆: 230733 Fax:
  (04865) 230933
- **B-Six Holiday Resort (P) Ltd.**
  ✆: 230527 Fax: 230193 Email:
  bsixresorts@md3.nsnl.net.in

- **Royal Retreat** ✆: 230440 Fax:
  230440, 231112
- **Edassery East End Hotel**
  ✆: 230451 Fax: 230227
- **Elseem Garden** ✆: 230510
- **The Residency** ✆: 230501 Fax:
  230265
- **Surya Ayurvedic Resort**
  ✆: 263204 Fax: (0487) 231347
  Email:surya@ayurveda
  resorts.com
- **Poopada Tourist Home**
  ✆: 230223, 231781
- **Spring Dale Resorts** ✆: 264268
- **Misha Tourist Home** ✆: 230376
- **Holiday Inn** ✆: 263204
- **Tourist Home Accommodation**
  ✆: 222506, 222229, 222179,
  222196, 222177, 222661

Kumily (STD: 04869)

- **Shalimar Spice Garden Resort**
  ✆: 222132 Fax: 223022
  Email:shalimarresort@vsnl.com
- **Michael's Inn** ✆: 222355 Fax:
  222356 Email:bvlpala@
  md3.vsnl.net.in
- **Tabernacle** ✆: 222240 Fax:
  222240
- **Revathy International**
  ✆: 222434 Fax: 222436
  Email:rissas@vsnl.com
- **Lissiya International**
  ✆: 223588 Fax: 223588
  Email:hotellissiya@usa.net.in
- **Mukkumckal Regent Tower**
  ✆: 222570 Fax: 223270
  Email:regenttower@hotmail.com
- **Homestays** ✆: 222229, 222547,
  222179, 222196

Others

- **Carmelia Haven, Vandanmedu**
  ✆: 270252 Fax: 04868-270268
- **Edassery Resorts, Kattapana**
  ✆: 272001 Fax: 04868-272712
- **Idukki Tower, Thodupuzha**
  ✆: 2224193 Fax: 04862-2224196
- **Gemini Tourist Home, Thodupuzha** ✆: 222734 Fax: 224364

Kozhikode

Facts and Figures

Area : 2,345 Sq.kms.
● Population : 2,878,498 (2001 census) ● Headquarters : Kozhikode ● Tourist Season: September to May.

Kozhikode, formerly known as Calicut, a typical English nomenclature, gains historic importance for, among a number of diverse reasons, it is the very spot where the great explorer Vasco-da-Gama landed in 1498 AD. It was once the capital of Zamorins.

Kozhikode district is bounded on the north by Kannur district, on the east by Wynad district, on the west by Arabian Sea.

Rivers: The important rivers of the district are the Mahe river, the Kuttiady river, the Korapuzha river, the Kallai river, the Chaliyar river and the Kadalundi river. The Chaliyar river is one the major rivers of the State.

The district is gifted with natural wonders and artificial splendours. The Museum and Art Gallery here is a treasure of antique furniture and objects d'art. There are excellent boating resorts. The importance given to science, engineering and technology is apparent from the 'Regional Science Centre'. The famous 'Kozhikode Planetarium' is a source of copious arrangement. The beach resorts and the ghat sections of the district are the favourite hangouts of both the locals and the visitors. The temples of the region adorn history.

Thus places of diverse interests are dissipated all over the district which as a whole helps enhance tourism.

Air: Kozhikode Airport is at Karipur, 23 km from city centre.

Rail: Kozhikode railway station is linked with major cities in the country.

In and Around Kozhikode

Srikandeswara Swamy Temple: This temple in the heart of the city is dedicated to Lord Siva. The famous Sivarathri festival is celebrated for seven days here.

Thacholi Manikkoth Temple: Situated 2 km from Vadakara, which is about 48 km from Kozhikode, this temple is dedicated to Thacholi Othenan, the paragon of martial arts. The 'Kalaripayattu' the deftful form of the art advocated by Him has set off a tradition which is much in vogue even today. This is also the birth place of the legend.

Thali Siva Temple: About 2 km from Vadakara, this temple dedicated to Lord Siva built by the Zamorian Swamy Thirumulpad is a structure of the 14th century architectural excellence. 'Revathi Pattathanam', the annual cultural event with its cognate intellectual features is indeed a discourse in Sanskrit, the India's ancient and one of the world's first languages. The temple celebrates an eight day festival every year.

Lokarnarkavu Bhagawathy Temple: At about 6 km on the east of Vadakara, in the place called Memunda, this temple is dedicated to Goddess Badrakali, the Goddess of bravery. Another example of a splendid architecture, the temple's walls, portray ancient paintings and carvings. The 41 day Mandala Vilakku festival is famous here.

Pazhassiraja Museum and Art Gallery: About 5 km off Kozhikode, this remarkable repository of ancient murals, antique bronzes, ancient coins excavated earthenware, temple models, stone umbrellas, condescends to the present an awesome picture of a glorious past. The Art Gallery abutting the Museum brandishes with pride the much admired paintings of Raja Ravi Varma and Raja Raja Varma.

Visiting Hours : 09.00-16.30 hrs (Closed on Mondays and other public holidays)

Krishna Menon Museum: A wing of this museum which is embellished by the evergreen paintings of Raja Ravi Varma and Raja Raja Varma, is set apart for the paraphernalia of V.K. Krishna Menon, the renowned statesman.

Kalipoika: 2 km from Kozhikode, this place offers an exciting boating experience.

Boating Hours: 8:00-19:00 hrs.

Kailai: The beautiful bridge of steel built by the British here, has stood the weather. This was once an important trading centre of Timber.

Kirtads: About 7 km from Kozhikode, the Museum contains ancient tools and devices of the tribal ancestors of Kerala. Anthropology and Sociology books are predominant in the library here.

Beypore: This place about 10 km South of Kozhikode, at

Chaliyar river-mouth was an important port and fishing harbour of the olden times. The 'Uru' or the 'Arabian Trading Vessel' here is one of the by-products of a 1500 years old tradition.

Kappad: This place, 16 km from Kozhikode, commands a place in the pages of history as it is here

that the great explorer Vasco-da-Gama set foot on Indian soil along with 170 assistants in three vessels on the 27th of May, 1498. The local name of the rocky beach is Kappakadavu. The temple on a rock here which protrudes into the sea, is believed to have been built about 800 years ago.

Kozhikode Beach: It is a pleasure to watch the Sunset from here. The old lighthouse and the two piers leaping into the sea each of which is over a hundred years old, the lions park for kids and the marine aquarium for the kids and the grown-ups alike, all add to the pleasure.

Velliyamkallu: The massive rock here forbade the Portuguese invaders as it offered the ideal footage to the Marrakas to counter attack the intruders. Once, the entire crew of a Portuguese warship was annihilated here. The rock with natural engravings is a real excitement.

Thikkolti Lighthouse: This lighthouse was necessiated as a ship, once, led off course had hit the shore. The tragic remains of the ship wreck can still be found. This region around the Velliyamkallu rock also serves as temporary halt for flight-weary, migratory birds.

Payyoli: This is again a beautiful beach, a favourite haunt of solitude-seekers, near Velliyamkallu.

Kadalaudi Bird Sanctuary: Exotic species of birds make their homes, between November and April at this river-mouth region. Terns, gulls, whimbrels, etc., are among those fascinating birds.

Planetarium: Located at Jaffarkhan Colony the planetarium seems to comprehend the prolific universe under one roof. The viewers are elevated to an utopian

State of being lost in the mystery of the Universe.

Show Hours: 12:00, 14:00, 16:00 and 18:00 hrs.

Regional Science Centre: Rubbing shoulders, with the 'Planetarium', the Science Centre provides an insight into the thrilling traits of 'Science'.

Kakkayam: About 45 km from Kozhikode, the beautiful dam amidst an enthralling landscape inundated with rare flora and fauna appeals not only to common tourists, but also to trekkers and rock climbers. The ideal season for an exciting visit is from November to April.

Tusharagiri: About 50 km from Kozhikode, the place is rich in rubber, arecanut, pepper and spice productions. The entire region, a trekker's attraction, is marked by excellent flora and fauna.

Two streams originating from the Western Ghats meet here to form the Challipuzha river. The river diverges into three waterfalls creating a snowy spray which gives the name Thusharagiri or the *'Snowy Peak'*. Of the three, the highest waterfall is the *Thenpara* that drops 75 metres.

Thiruvangoor Sree Maha-ganapathy Temple, Kozhikode: This temple dedicated to *Lord Ganapathy* - the elephant-headed son of Lord Siva, is located at Thiruvangoor, 18 km from Kozhikode. The annual festival *'Sivarathri Utsavam'* of the temple lasts for two days. *Theyyam,* the ritual spectacle is performed on the second day watched by a large crowd of devotees, who at the end receive blessings in persons from the `Theyyam'.

Dolphin's Point: Here one can see in the early hours of the morning dolphins playing in the sea. The beach is 2 km from Kozhikode town .

Badagara: A commercial centre of *martial arts, Kalaripayattu.* Badagara, 48 km from Kozhikode is also the birthplace of *Tacholi Othenan,* whose heroic deeds have been immortalised in the ballads of North Malabar.

Peruvannamuzhi: 60 km from Kozhikode, the place has more than one reason to be proud of. The beautiful dam surrounded by

picturesque hills, the serene reservoir with boating facilities, the tranquil islands free of inhabitants, the bird sanctuary wherein a large species of inhabitant and migratory birds greet each other and a crocodile farm of the occasionally sprinting and otherwise sluggish creatures, all make the experience thrilling and unforgettable. `Samaraka-thottam', a garden commemo rating the freedom-fighters of the

region can also be seen.

Vellari Mala: The verdant landscape, with a beauty of its own, holds aloft a sparkling waterfalls. Trekkers are naturally attracted here.

Kuttiyadi: This beautiful village is situated 78 km from Kozhikode. This is the site of Kuttiyadi Hydro-electric Power Project.

Iringal: This place is of archaeological importance. Kunjali Marikkar, the commander of Zamorians Naval fleet, who defied the Portuguese vessels for a long time, was born here on the banks of the river `Moorad' and the site is now under preservation by the Dept. of Archaeology.

Mananchira Maidan: The king Mana Vikrama is ever remembered for the marvellous architecture on the palace tank. Traditional Kerala style is reflected on the buildings around the captivating musical fountain and the conscientiously cut lawns here.

Kuttichira: The Maccunthi Mosque here and other old Mosques in Kozhikode strike a stunning similarity in construction and architecture with that of the Hindu temples. The stone inscriptions of the Muccunthi Mosques unravel interesting vignettes of the Zamorins and their patronage of Islam.

Mishkal Masjid: This is again one of the oldest Mosques of Kuttichira. It has four storeys and sturdy wooden pillars. Rich in architecture, some parts of the

Mosque had been burnt down by the Portuguese in 1510 and the charred remains can still be seen. The mosque owes the origin of its name to the rich trader who built it.

Pishakarikavu: Goddess Bhagavathy is the presiding deity of this temple. Elephant pageants are part of the celebrations of the annual festival in March/April.

Mannur Temple: 12 km from Kozhikode, the temple resembles the one dedicated to Lord Siva at Thiruvannur. The 'Gajaprathishta' of laterite structure here is over 200 years old. The legend has it that, Sri Parasuraman starts his 'Siva Linga Prathishta' at Thirvannur and finishes it here. Hence, the poojas at noon are of particular importance. The annual festival, 'Sivarathri' is famous here.

Ponneri: The ritzy paintings of the Sri Krishna temple and the Siva temple at Karatt and Ponneri respectively portray incidences from the 'Puranas'.

Varakkal Devi Temple: Parasurama, according to the legends, the creator of Kerala, ploughed this area out of divine intuition when Goddess Devi with all Her Mercy appeared before him. This is considered to be the last of the 108 temples built by Sri Parasurama. 'Vavu Bali' during which thousands perform ancestral obsequies is the main festival here. The benevolent sea remains amazingly calm as the people carry out the rites.

Jain Temple: The two temples at the Trikkovil lane are known for their beautiful paintings and wonderful porticos.

Parsi Anju Amman Bang: This is a 'Fire Temple' on the S.M. Street. The temple is two centuries old and was built during the early Parsi settlements.

Buddha Vihar: This temple of both historic and religious interest has a number of books on the birth, life and teachings of 'The Buddha'.

Muchunthi Palli: This is a beautiful mosque of the grand traditional style of Kerala architecture. The donations to the mosque by a Zamorian is learnt from the 13th century inscription on a stone slab, 'Vattezhuthu'.

Mother of God Church: This church built in 1513 AD is an architectural splendour of the grand Roman style, the like of which can hardly be found elsewhere in Kerala. The church also has a 2 century old portait of St. Mary. It is a famous pilgrim centre.

The lagoons of Kozhikode: The backwaters of Kozhikode are thrilling holiday resorts. The estuaries, as fascinating as ever with boating facilities attract a large number of tourists. There are exciting boat house cruises to be relished.

Malabar House Boat Cruise: For details contact Mavila Resorts. Ph : 0495 - 2352447 Fax : 2352547 Mobile : 94470 12447

For package tours contact: DTPC, District Collectorate, Kozhikode, Ph. : 2720012 Fax : 2370582

Festivals

Malabar Mahotsavam: This is a grand festival of the Malabar region celebrated with much rejoice characterised by the confluence of traditional and cultural art performances. It falls between January and February every year.

Sivarathri: It is a grand affair at Sreekanteswara Temple. Ardent devotees with profound belief fast all day and perform Poojas to Lord Siva all through the night of the Sivarathri day. It occurs in the month of February.

Jalotsavam: Water fiestas are the highlight of the festival. It is held between February and March by the sports clubs at Korapuzha, Pongilodippara. This is a part of the grand Onam festival.

Tourist Information Offices

- **Kozhikode Railway Station**
  ✆ : 91-495-2702606
- **Karipur Airport** ✆ : 91-483-2712762
- **DTPC** ✆ : 91-495-2720012 Fax: 91-495-2370582

Accommodation

Kozhikode (STD: 0495)

- **Fortune Hotel** ✆: 2768888 Fax: 2768111
- **Taj Residency (5 Star)** ✆: 2765354 Fax: 2766448 **Email**:rajclt@md3.vsnl.net.in
- **Kappad Beach Resort** ✆: 2683760 Fax: 2683706 **Email**: moosa@kappadbeachresort.com
- **Hotel Malabar Palace** ✆: 2721511 Fax: 2721794
- **Hotel Sea Queen** ✆: 2366604 Fax: 2365854
- **Hotel Hyson** ✆: 2766423 Fax: 2766518
- **Calicut Towers** ✆: 2723202 Fax: 2720702
- **Hotel Regency** ✆: 2723121 Fax: 2722694
- **Aradhana Tourist Home** ✆: 2302021 Fax: 2302220
- **Metro Towers** ✆: 2700571 Fax: 2301647
- **Malabar Mansion** ✆: 2722391 Fax: 2721593
- **Hotel Maharani** ✆: 2723101
- **Sasthapuri Tourist Home** ✆: 2723281 Fax: 2721543 **Email**:sasthapuri@md4.vsnl.net.in
- **Kalpaka Tourist Home** ✆: 2720222 Fax: 2720222
- **DTPC, District Collectorate, Kozhikode** ✆: 2720012 Fax: 2370582

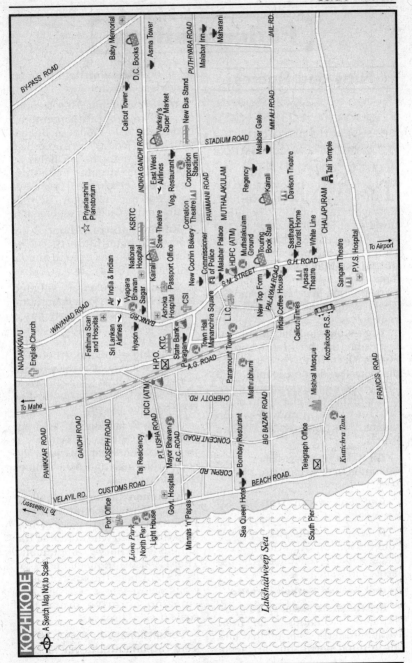

KOZHIKODE

A Sketch Map Not to Scale.

Pathanamthitta

Facts and Figures

Area   :   2,642   Sq.kms.
• Population : 1,231,577 (2001 census) • Headquarters : Pathanamthitta • Tourist Season: August to March.

This forms the neighbour to the three districts Kollam, Kottayam and Idukki. There is a number of temples including the Lord Ayyappa at Sabarimala where thousands of pilgrims throng during the Makara Jothi festival. The birth place of historic personalities like Muloor and Sri Shakli Badra render honour to the region.

Rivers: Achan Kovil, Manimala and Pamba are the three important rivers that flow through this district. The second Pamba river merges beautifully with two other rivers giving the place, the name 'Thriveni Sangamam' which means 'The Confluence of Three Rivers'.

Air: The nearest airport is at Nedumbassery, Ernakulam 146 km away.

Rail: Rail link at Tiruvalla, 30 km away.

It is in this district, a huge convention of Christians takes place, which is reckoned to be the largest in Asia.

In and Around Pathanamthitta

Rakthakanta Swamy Temple: Situated in Omallur, 5 km from Pathanamthitta, this temple and the annual cattle fair attract a large number of visitors from far and wide.

Malayalapuzha: This temple, about 8 km from Pathanamthitta is dedicated to Goddess Bhagavathy. The Goddess here according to the prevalent belief, helps all the genuine dreams of faithful devotees come true. The mural paintings and excellent carvings of the temple are a visual feast.

Kadammanitta: About 8 km from Pathanamthitta, this Devi Temple celebrates a grand annual festival for 10 days in April/May.

Konni: This place is situated about 11 km from Pathanamthitta. This agricultural region has a bounty of rubber, pepper, coffee, ginger, etc. It is also the centre for training elephants where the magnificent beings of the wild are tamed and trained for useful work. Elephant is the much sought after entertainment here.

Mulour Smarakam: 12 km from Pathanamthitta, stands a memorial built after the renowned social reformer and poet Muloor at Elavamthitta.

Kodumon Chilanthiambalam: 15 km from Pathanamthitta, Kodumon is the birth place of Sree Shakthi Bhadra who authored the famous 'Aascharya Chudamani'. There is also a temple famous for its well, 'Chilanthi kinar' (spider well), whose water, it is said, has amazing curative properties against skin diseases.

Perunthenaruvi: About 36 km from Pathanamthitta via Vachoochira the splendid waterfalls situated on the banks of the sacred river Pamba is as much an attraction to tourists from abroad as to those from within.

Sabarimala: It is located at about 72 km from Pathanamthitta town, 191 km from Thiruvananthapuram and 210 km from Kochi. It is here the famous temple dedicated to Lord Ayyappa where thousand upon thousands of ardent devotees throng between the months November and January. The devotees undertake a vow for about 48 days during which period they stick to strict austerity before taking on the pilgrimage. The tranquil temple situated in the picturesque mountain ranges of Sabarimala, at about 914 m above sea level, which can be reached only on foot traversing about 4 km remains closed on all other days of the year except during the festive season between November and January and the first five days of every 'Malayalam' month and also during Vishu. The nearest railway station Thiruvalla is about 102 km away. The temple welcomes people of all castes and creeds; however, women between 10 and 50 years are not allowed inside.

Pamba: It is the major halt of pilgrims on the way to Sabarimala. A holy dip in the sacred waters of the river is customary among the pilgrims. The place is also known as 'Thriveni Sangamam' which means 'The Confluence of Three Rivers'.

Aranmula: About 10 km from the nearest railway station, Chengannur, 'The Parthasarathy Temple' here is dedicated to Lord Krishna. The sacred Pamba river flows by the temple. As a conclusive part of the popular Onam Festival, a boat race is conducted. The 'Vijnana Kalavedi' here is the centre for learning traditional arts like the Kathakali, classical music and dance as well as Kalaripayattu. The Parthasarathy Temple also has 18th century murals. A number of foreigners can be seen making a long stay to get an unadulterated idea of the fathomless depths of the rich traditions of Kerala.

Aranmula is famed for its hand made mirrors of polished metal called 'Aranmula Kannadi'.

Thiruvalla: The place is famed by the presence of Malankara Marthoma Syrian Church headquarters. The wall paintings of the Paliakara Church here are extraordinary. Kathakali performances are part of the daily routines in or probably only in the 'Sree Vallaba Temple' here.

Mannadi: The stone sculptures in the ancient Bagavathy temple are remarkable. This place, about 13 km from Adoor is where the renowned freedom fighter Veluthampi Dalawa who hailed from Travancore, spent his last days. This is also the venue of Folklore and Folk Arts Institute of Kerala. An annual festival is held between February and March.

Niranam: This place, 7 km from Thiruvalla, boasts of its famous poets and ancient church. The church, oldest in India, believed to have been built by apostle St.Thomas in 52 AD is situated here which is also the birth place of the poets and social reformers, popular as 'Kannassa Kavigal'.

Nilackal: Situated about 5 km from Plappally, this place is of reverence to both Hindus and Christians. The old Siva Temple is an important centre of worship for the Hindus. The Ecumenical centre of the Christians is also found here.The place is also the venue of the estate of 'Farming Corporation'.

Pandalam: This Holy town is about 14 km away from Chengannur railway station. The Valiakoikal temple on the banks of the river Achenkoil bears resemblance to the Lord Ayyappa Temple at Sabarimala. The pilgrims on their way to Sabarimala customarily worship here since this is the place, according to the legends, where Lord Ayyappa, on his human incarnation, was born as the son of the King of Pandalam. As part of the festival formalities, the sacred ornaments of the Lord Sri Ayyappa are taken in a grand procession, teemed with ardent devotees, from here to Sabarimala, three days in advance of the famous 'Holy Makaravilakku festival'.

Parumala: About 10 km from 'Thiruvalla', the place is known for the grand festival 'Ormaperunal' which means 'Commemoration day'. It is the commemoration of 'Mar Gregorios Metropolitan', the declared saint of Malankara Orthodox Church, celebrated on the 1st and 2nd of November every year.

Charalkunnu: This piquant picnic spot is a picturesque hill station from where the breath-taking areal view of the beautiful valleys and other low lying lands can easily knock any one out of one's senses. The camp house here offers a feel-at-home lodging.

Cherukolpuzha: This is the place where thousands of Hindus congregate, usually in February every year and perform an important religious ritual on the river bed of the Holy Pamba.

Kakki Reservoir: The vast sheet of the serene waters is ideally encapsuled by a verdant expanse of thick forests which are homes to a number of dangerously beautiful tigers, magnificently attractive elephants and ostensibly human monkeys which can at times be sighted.

Kaviyoor: About 5 km east of Thiruvalla, overseeing the delightful Manimala river, Kaviyoor has a small hillock on which stands the gravel Hanuman Temple, dedicated to 'Lord Anjeneya', in which the marvellous triangular structures and also the rest of the wonderful architecture are much different from the usual Kerala style of splendid architecture. Just about half a kilometre from here there is yet another architectural marvel, the rock cut Siva Temple. The tranquil temple belongs to the 8th century and reflects the great Pallava architecture.

Manjanikara: Mar Ignatius Elias III, the clergy and patriot of Anthiod, on his errand to India, breathed his last here in the year 1932. His mortal remains are preserved in the church here. This place, in course of time has turned into a famous pilgrim centre. 'Ormaperunal' the annual festival is celebrated in February.

Maramon: This place is the Holy site of the christians where thousands of them from all over the world congregate for a huge religious convention. The clergy and evangelists of different parts of the world address the convention which is held in February. This is perhaps the christian convention of maximum turnout in the whole of Asia.

Vijnana Kala Vedi Cultural Centre: Vijnana Kala Vedi Cultural Centre founded by *Louba Schild,* a French scholar under the Indo French Cultural Exchange Programme, was started with UNESCO support. Those interested in culture and the arts would not want to miss it. The centre offers residential training courses in Kerala's traditional arts and crafts like *Kathakali, Mohiniattam, Bharata Natyam, Kalaripayattu, Music, Wood carving,* etc.

Festivals

The cattle fair and the annual 10 day festival at Rakthakanta Swamy Temple and Devi Temple are celebrated with much fanfare.

The Makara Jothi festival at Sabarimala, between November and January is a grand one teeming with devotees from far and wide, drenched in devotion.

The boat races mark the conclusion of the grand Onam festival with a competitive and yet a congenial note.

The mammoth christian religious convention considered to be the largest in the whole of Asia welcomes devotees from all over the world.

Tourist Information Office

- **Tourist Information Office,** ✆: 91-468-2326409

- **DTPC Office,** ✆:91-468-2229952
- **Devaswom Information Centre,** Pamba ✆: 91-4735-203339
- **Devaswom Guest House,** Sabarimala ✆: 91-4735-202056
- **Devaswom Information Centre,** Sabarimala ✆: 91-4735-202048

Accommodation

Pathanamthitta (STD: 0468)
- **Hotel May Fair** ✆: 2322894
- **Ashoka International** ✆: 2324927
- **Hotel Dolphin** ✆: 2323220 Fax: 2325661

Adoor (STD: 04734)
- **Apsara Tourist Home,** M.C. Road.
- **Fathima Tourist Home,** Pathanamthitta Road.
- **Adoor Tourist Home,** Central Jn.
- **Amritha Tourist Home,** Central Jn.

Pandalam (STD: 04734)
- **Hotel Shimi's,** M.C. Road.
- **S.N. Tourist Home,** M.C. Road.
- **Suni Tourist Home,** Medical Mission Jn.

Ranni (STD: 04735)
- **Sree Ayyappa Tourist Home,** Main Road.
- **Karakath Tourist Home,** Pazhavangadi Jn.
- **Mammukku Kalpana Tourist Home,** Pazhavangadi

Kozhencherry (STD: 0468)
- **Mothi Tourist Home,** Central Jn.

Mallapally (STD: 04738)
- **Hotel Sea Blue,** Near Private Bus Stand.

Thiruvalla (STD: 04736)
- **Hotel Panchamai,** Railway Station Road.
- **Hotel Elite,** M.C. Road.
- **Hotel Asoka,** T.K. Road.

Ernakulam

Facts and Figures

Area : 2,408 Sq.kms.
● Population : 3,098,378 (2001 census) ● Headquarters : Kochi ● Tourist Season: September to May.

This is again a land of lavish legends and legacies. The towns of Ernakulam and Kochi, the almost inseparable twins, brandish ancient movements, places of historical significance and a number of ancient temples. The ancient Portugal and Dutch monuments and the early British structures are reminiscent of a glorious sequence of historical events. The colossal places of the Maharajas (Kings) of the region speak volumes of the rich architecture of the part. 'Kaladi', the birth place of the great Hindu philosopher Adi Sankarar, who promulgated the doctrine of 'Advaitha' which means 'Not Two But One', is situated in this district. Unique legends and conventions are associated with the temples and churches of the region.

The entire region is gifted with natural landscapes of enormous beauty. The sumptuous sanctuaries swarmed with capricious birds are a delight to the sight. The bird sanctuary at Thottakadu is also home to certain wildlife creatures.

Thus, this part of Kerala is always full of joyous visitors everywhere.

Rivers: Periyar and Murattu-puzha are the main rivers of the district. The Chalakudi river which flows through north of Alwaye also joins Periyar at Alanthikara. The rivers of Thodupuzha, Kallai and Kothamangalam join together to form Muvattupuzha rivers.

Air: Cochin International Airport is at Nedumbassery, 33 km North east of Ernakulam city.

Rail: Kochi is connected by rail with many important cities.

Ferry: The main Ferry Station (Boat jetty) is located 1 k.m. away from Ernakulam South Railway Station. From here, boats are available to all islands.

In and Around Ernakulam

Pierce Leslie Bungalow: This grand edifice was the office of Pierce Leslie & Co., the centuries old coffee merchants, in 1862. The style of the construction seems to be the rare outcome of the fusion of three great architectural excellences - the Dutch, the Portuguese and the last but not the least, the Keralite. The verandahs are furnished with waterfronts.

Koder House: This is again an 18th century edifice of elegance built by Samuel S. Koder of the Kochin Electric Company. The architecture here emphasises the advent of Indo-European style over the colonial style.

Delta study: The High School here is part of the magnificent bungalow built in 1808 which was once a warehouse.

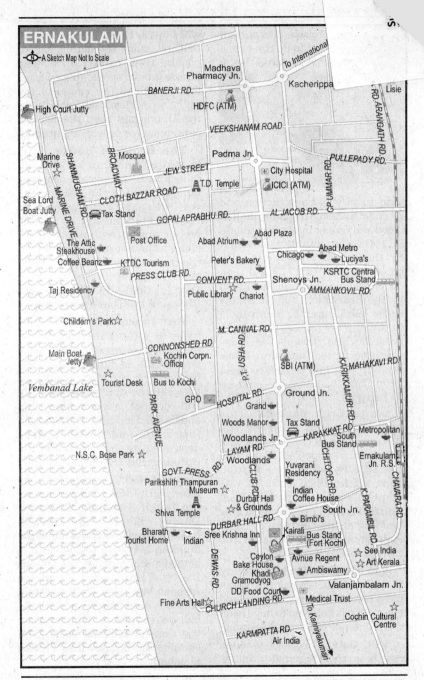

ERNAKULAM

A Sketch Map Not to Scale

Madhava Pharmacy Jn.

To International

BANERJI RD.

Kacherippa

Lisie

High Court Jutty

HDFC (ATM)

RD. ARANGATH RD.

VEEKSHANAM ROAD

Marine Drive

Mosque

BROADWAY

Padma Jn.

PULLEPADY RD.

JEW STREET

City Hospital

Sea Lord Boat Jutty

CLOTH BAZZAR ROAD

T.D. Temple

ICICI (ATM)

CP UMMAR RD.

MARINE DRIVE RD.

Tax Stand

GOPALAPRABHU RD.

AL JACOB RD.

SHANMUGHAM RD.

The Attic Steakhouse

Post Office

Abad Atrium

Abad Plaza

Coffee Beanz

KTDC Tourism

Peter's Bakery

Chicago

Abad Metro

Luciya's

PRESS CLUB RD.

CONVENT RD.

Shenoys Jn.

KSRTC Central Bus Stand

Taj Residency

Public Library

Chariot

AMMANKOVIL RD.

Childern's Park

M. CANNAL RD.

CONNONSHED RD.

Main Boat Jetty

Kochin Corpn. Office

P.T. USHA RD.

SBI (ATM)

MAHAKAVI RD.

Tourist Desk

Bus to Kochi

Vembanad Lake

GPO

HOSPITAL RD.

Ground Jn.

KARIKKAMURI RD.

PARK AVENUE

Grand

N.S.C. Bose Park

Woods Manor

Tax Stand

KARAKKAT RD.

Metropolitan

Woodlands Jn.

South Bus Stand

LAYAM RD.

ACHTOOR RD.

Ernakulam Jn. R.S.

Woodlands

GOVT. PRESS. RD.

Yuvarani Residency

Parikshith Thampuran Museum

CLUB RD.

Indian Coffee House

CHAVARA RD.

Shiva Temple

Durbar Hall & Grounds

South Jn.

Bharath Tourist Home

DURBAR HALL RD.

Bimbi's

Sree Krishna Inn

Kairali

Indian

Bus Stand (Fort Kochi)

DEWAS RD.

Ceylon Bake House

Avnue Regent

See India

Art Kerala

Khadi Gramodyog

Ambiswamy

K.PARAMBIL RD.

Fine Arts Hall

DD Food Court

Valanjambalam Jn.

CHURCH LANDING RD.

Medical Trust

Cochin Cultural Centre

KARMPATTA RD.

Air India

To Kanniyakumari

St. Francis Church: This ancient church, reckoned to be the oldest European church in India, has a

long history of construction and re-construction. Originally built of wood and timber by the Portuguese in 1503, the church was rebuilt by the Dutch protestants with stone masonry in 1779 and then converted into an Anglican church by the British in 1795. It is now under the Church of South India Council. The tombstone of the great historic voyager Vasco-da-Gama can be seen here since it was here he was laid to rest in 1524 before his remains were removed to Portugal.

Santa Cruz Basilica: This ancient church built by the Portuguese was consecrated as a Cathedral by Pope Paul IV in1558. Eventually, when the British annexed Kochi in 1795, it was demolished. Then Bishop Dom Gomez Ferreira established a new building at the very site in 1887. Pope John Paul II declared the church, Basilica in1894.

Vasco House: This 16th century building with typical European glass paned windows, balcony and verandahs is believed to have been the residence of Vasco-da-Gama.

VOC Gate: This huge wooden gate in front of the parade grounds was built in 1740. The monogram VOC by which the gate is called, can be seen carved on it. The parade ground spreads over 4 acres and was once the venue of the military parades of the Portuguese, the Dutch and then the British. Now, it serves as a sports ground.

The Bishop's House: This beautiful building on a small hillock near the parade grounds, built in 1506 as the residence of the Portuguese Governor has its facelift embellished by Gothic arches and a tread-worthy path along a circular garden leading to the inviting portal. The building then went into the possession of Dom Jos Gomes Ferreira, the 27th Bishop of the Diocese of Kochi.

Fort Immanuel: What looks today as a reticent remnant of a mighty structure along the beach was once a magnificent fort. The bastion here signified the alliance between the then rulers of Kochi and Portugal. It was built in 1503 and fortified in 1538. The beautiful fort walls and bastions were destroyed by the Dutch and the British in the 1800's and after.

David Hall: It was built in the later part of the 17th century by the Dutch East India Company. David Koder, a Jewish businessman, by whose name the building is known today was one of the later occupants. The famous Dutch Commander Hendrick Ardiaan Van Reed Tot Drakestein who was originally linked with the hall was the pioneer who compiled the flora of Malabar coast. The compilation is known as Hortus Malabaricus.

The Cochin Club: It started functioning in the 1900's. The club houses an impressive collection of sporting trophies. It is situated in a meticulously beautified park.

Mattancherry Palace: Also known as the Dutch Palace, this

beautiful structure renovated by the Dutch in 1663 was originally built by the Portuguese in 1557 and presented to Raja Veera Kerala Varma of Kochi. Today, it is a 'Portrait Gallery' of Kochi Rajas. There are beautiful wall paintings here. Old Dutch maps of Kochi, royal palanquins and other ancient materials add to the attraction.

Visiting Hours : 10:00 to 17:00 hrs. Closed on Fridays.

Synagogue: Built in 1568, this is the oldest synagogue in the Commonwealth. It was destroyed in 1662 during the Portuguese raid and rebuilt after 2 years by the Dutch. Among the exquisite elements are a clock tower, stone slabs with Hebrew inscriptions,

great scrolls of Old Testament, copper plates bearing ancient scripts, etc.

The floor tiles here are willow patterned and hand painted of the 18th century China style, brought from Canton.

Visiting Hours: 10:00 - 12:00 hrs. and 15:00 - 17:00 hrs. Closed on Fridays, Saturdays and Jewish Holidays.

Jew Town: The area around the synagogue is known as Jew Town. It is the centre of spice trade and curio shops.

Cherai Beach: This beautiful beach along the border of the placid island Vypeen is ideal for swimming. The maritime friend of humans, the Dolphins can occasionally be sighted. Paddy fields and coconut groves are abundant.

Bolgatty Island: This wonderful holiday resort is where the Bolghatty Palace was built in 1744 by the Dutch which was then taken over by the British. Now, it serves as a hotel managed by the K.T.D.C. A small golf course and honeymoon cottages are special features.

Gundu Island: With an area of 5 acres, Gundu Island is the smallest island around Cochin.

Wellingdon Island: This artificial island in the middle of the artful backwaters is named after Lord Willingdon, a former British Viceroy of India. There are in this beautiful place, excellent hotels, trading centres, Port Trust and the Southern Naval Command Headquarters.

The Hill Palace Museum: Located at Thripunithura about 10 km from Kochi, this beautiful palace was built in 1865. This huge palace is constituted by as many as 49 extravagant buildings of traditional architectural style of Kerala. The palace has benevolently made room for an outstanding Museum in which one can relish the glory of 19th century paintings, murals, stone sculptures, manuscripts, inscriptions and a lot more. The vast area of 52 acres of terraced land around the palace has to its credit deer parks and horse riding facilities. Tripunithura is also known for the nearby Chottanikara temple and Poornathraessa temple.

Parikshith Thampuran Museum: A good number of ancient coins, bronzes, copies of murals and megalithic relics of Kerala are on display here. It is adjacent to the Shiva temple on Darbar Hall Road, Ernakulam.

Madhavan Nayar Foundation: Found in this exclusive foundation, which is about 8 km from Ernakulam town, at Edapally are life size figures revealing the historic episodes and events from the neolithic to the neoteric era. The gallery exclusive to paintings and sculptures displays more than 200 original works of the contemporary Indian artists. Among the visual arts collection are authentic reproduction of certain world masters and mural reproductions of Indian art which are larger than life size. The light and sound shows with English and Malayalam commentaries attract a number of visitors.

Vamanamoorthy Temple: This temple dedicated to Lord Vamana, one of the divine incarnations of

Lord Vishnu has inscriptions spanning over three centuries from the 10th to the 13th. The deity is popularly known as 'Thrikka-kariappan'. A 10 day festival is celebrated here.

Kaladi: About 32 km from Ernakulam, this place is elated to divine honours by the birth of the great philosopher and reformer of Hinduism, Adi Sankara. The place is also sanctified by the temples dedicated to Sri Sankara, Sarada Devi, Sri Krishna and Sri Ramakrishna. According to the legends, Sankara's mother Aryamba was turning down his repeated pleas to take up austerity when one fine day a crocodile caught his feet and held on until he convinced his mother and obtained her permission. The legendary spot called 'Crocodile Ghat' can also be seen.

Kodanad: It is one of the largest elephant training centres of South India. On the north of the place flows the beautiful river Periyar. The elephants are mainly trained for Safari. There is also a small zoo.

Chennamangalam: About 42 km from Ernakulam, this is a place of versatile landscape. Three beautiful rivers, one more than a half a dozen inlets, picturesque hillocks and gleeming plains of green vastness all form a rare and a rapturous combination. The Paliam Palace here representing the splendid architecture of Kerala was the official residence of the Paliath Achaus, the hereditary prime ministers to the Kings of Kochi. Many historic documents and important relics are preserved here. The noble ideal of peaceful coexistence of religions is well exemplified by the unusual presence of a temple, a church, a mosque and also a synagogue, congenially close to one another all of which can be viewed with reverence from the enthralling hillocks at Kottayil Kovilakom. The remains of the Vypeenkotta Seminary built by the Portuguese in the 16th century keeps the onlookers guessing about its wholesome grandeur.

Malayatoor: Situated about 47 km from Kochi, the place is sanctified by the presence of a Catholic church on a beautiful hill, at an altitude of about 609 m. The church, dedicated to St. Thomas receives thousands of dedicated devotees during the annual festival–Malayatoor Perunal between March and April. The Holy Saint Thomas is believed to have prayed here.

Bhothathankettu: An excellent picnic spot about 50 km northeast of Ernakulam town embedded in a vast expanse of virgin forest

which is just a short distance away from another spot of endless enjoyment, the 'Salim Ali Bird Sanctuary' at Thattakkadu at Bhothathankettu is situated near the two main irrigation projects, the Periyar Valley and the Idamalayar Irrigation projects. It

is also a trekkers' paradise. Nearest railway station: Ernakulam Junction, about 50 km away. Nearest airport: Kochi International Airport about 26 km from Ernakulam town.

Thattakkadu Bird Sanctuary: On the Kochi-Munnar road, about 20 km from Kothamangalam this

scintillating sanctuary is rightly named after its discoverer Dr.Salim Ali, the renowned ornithologist. The Salim Ali Sanctuary holds a variety of native birds like the Malabar grey-horn bill, the woodpecker, the parakeet and so on. The Ceylon frog-moth and rose-billed roller are among the rare birds. A large variety of migrant birds makes itself comfortable during the season here. With luck, one can also sight wildlife.Nearest railway station : Aluva, about 48 km away. Nearest airport : Cochin International Airport, about 44 km.

Chinese Fishing Nets: The

entrance to the Cochin harbour is dotted by the Chinese Fishing Nets called Cheena Vala in Malayalam. There are large nets which hang from bamboo or teak posts and are still used by local fishermen in Fort Cochin to catch fish attracted by the lights suspended above the net.

Munikkal Guhalayam: Located atop a hill at Chengamanad (30 kms north of Kochi), this is a place shrouded in mythology. It is believed that Sage Jangaman had lived here around 2000 years ago, and the place was initially known as Jangaman. A famous Lord Murugan temple is located on the spot where the sage is said to have meditated which was later consecrated by Chattambi Swamikal in 1898. The word 'Munikkal Guhalayam' literally means 'sages rock cave'. Another story goes that Lord Murugan also called as 'Guhalayam' had made this place as his abode and hence the word 'Guhalayam'.

In and Around Kochi

Siva Temple: This temple is dedicated to Lord Siva. The presiding deity here, one of the various forms of the Lord, is known as Ernakulathappan. An eight day annual festival is famous here.

Valanjambalam Devi Temple: This Devi temple celebrates a 2 day annual festival known as Thalapoli Utsavam marked by caprisoned elephant.

Sri Poornathraessa Temple: Lord Krishna is the presiding deity here. Three festivals are celebrated here in a grand manner.

'Athachamayam' the splendid procession on Atham which marks the beginning of the famous, long Onam festival is a beauty to watch.

Chakkamkulangara Siva Temple: Situated at Thirupuni-thura, this temple dedicated to Lord Siva celebrates the famous 'Sivarathri' festival for 7 days.

Mahadeva Temple: This temple situated at Nettur is dedicated to the Lord 'Sankara Narayana' who is indeed an interesting combination of Lord Siva and Lord Vishnu. It is 10 km from Ernakulam.

Baghavathy Temple: This Baghavathy Temple is situated at Thirupunithura. A seven day festival is famous here.

Sri Rajeswari Temple: This temple at Chottanikara follows a unique convention by which Goddess Saraswathi is worshipped in the morning, Goddess Badrakali at noon and Goddess Durga in the evening. The famous temple tank here is believed to act as an exorcist, as a dip in the holy tank drives away the evil spirits tormenting the possessed individuals.

Perumthrikoil Temple: Situated on the banks of the beautiful river Muvattupuzha near Piravom. The idol in this temple is made of river sand and the one winged Garuda, the mythical Eagle, carved in wood.

Bhagavathy Temple: This temple at Cheranallur is situated 12 km from Ernakulam. The temple hosts two annual festival of which one lasts for 9 days and the other for a day.

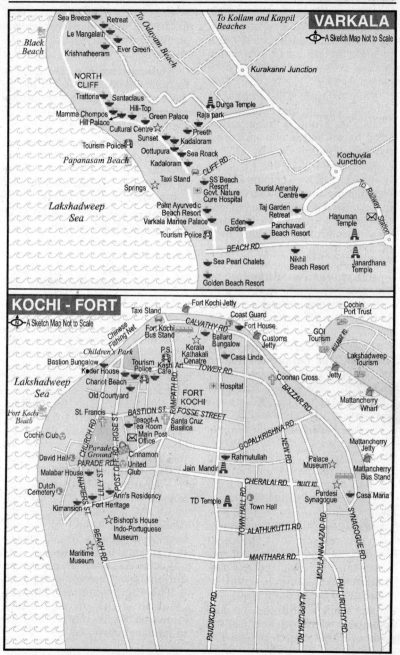

VARKALA

Sea Breeze · Retreat
Le Mangalath
Krishnatheeram · Ever Green

To Kollam and Kappil Beaches
Black Beach
To Odayam Beach
A Sketch Map Not to Scale

Kurakanni Junction

NORTH CLIFF
Trattoria · Santaclaus
Hill-Top
Mamma Chompos · Green Palace · Raja park
Hill Palace
Cultural Centre · Preeth
Sunset · Kadaloram
Tourism Police
Oottupura · Sea Roack
Kadaloram

Durga Temple

Papanasam Beach

CLIFF RD.

Kochuvila Junction

Taxi Stand
Springs
SS Beach Resort
Govt. Nature Cure Hospital
Tourist Amenity Centre
To Railway Station

Lakshadweep Sea

Palm Ayurvedic Beach Resort
Varkala Marine Palace
Taj Garden Retreat
Hanuman Temple

Tourism Police
Eden Garden
Panchavadi Beach Resort

BEACH RD.

Sea Pearl Chalets
Nikhil Beach Resort
Janardhana Temple

Golden Beach Resort

KOCHI - FORT

A Sketch Map Not to Scale

Taxi Stand
Fort Kochi Jetty
Coast Guard
Cochin Port Trust

CALVATHY RD.
Fort House
Customs Jetty
GOI Tourism

Chinese Fishing Net
Fort Kochi Bus Stand
Ballard Bungalow
Casa Linda
MULLER RD.
Lakshadweep Tourism

Children's Park
P.S.
Kerala Kathakali Cenatre
TOWER RD.

Bastion Bungalow
Koder House
Tourism Police
Kashi Art Cafe
Coonan Cross
Jetty

Lakshadweep Sea
Chariot Beach
Old Courtyard

FORT KOCHI
Hospital

Mattancherry Wharf

Fort Kochi Beach
St. Francis
BASTION ST.
FOSSE STREET
BAZZAR RD.

Mattancherry Jetty

Cochin Club
Teapot-A Tea Room
Santa Cruz Basilica
GOPALKRISHNA RD.

David Hall
Main Post Office
Cinnamon
Rahmutullah
NEW RD.
Palace Museum
Mattancherry Bus Stand

Malabar House
United Club
Jain Mandir
PALACE RD.
Casa Maria

Dutch Cemetery
CHERALAI RD.
Pardesi Synagogue

Arin's Residency
Fort Heritage
TD Temple
Town Hall
SYNAGOGUE RD.

Kimansion
Bishop's House
Indo-Portuguese Museum
ALATHUKUTTI RD.

PALURUTHY RD.

Maritime Museum
MANTHARA RD.

CHURCH ST.
ROSE ST.
PARADE RD.
Parade Ground
POST OFFICE ST.
LILLY ST.
NAPIER'S ST.
BEACH RD.
RAMPATH RD.
TOWN HALL RD.
PANDIKUDY RD.
ALAPPUZHA RD.
MOULANNAIZAD RD.

Mahadeva Temple: This temple, dedicated to Lord Siva is located 25 km from Ernakulam and hosts an eight day annual festival which comes to an end with Arattu celebrations.

Siva Temple: This temple at Alwaye has a unique feature. The Holy Siva Linga is installed on sand banks and is not enshrined in any Pagoda.

Mahadeva Temple: Situated between Thrikkariyoor and Kothamangalam, this temple dedicated to Lord Siva is one of the ancient temples. Kurathiyattam, Chakyarkoothu, Pathakam, etc., are parts of a grand 10 day annual festival.

Azhakiyakavu Bhagavathy Temple: This temple at Palluruthy celebrates a grand festival marked by sparkling fireworks for 22 days.

Thonnyakavu Bhagavathy Temple: This temple is situated at North Parur. An eight day festival marked by the 'Ezhunallathu', 'Elephant Processions' is celebrated.

Sri Venkatachalapathy Temple: In this temple at North Parur, dedicated to Lord Venkatachalapathy, one of the various forms of Lord Vishnu, a 6 day festival is celebrated in a grand way.

Mahadeva Temple: This temple at Vaikom is one of the most famous Siva temples. 'Annadhana' (feeding) is conducted here. Vaikom Ashtami festival is celebrated for 13 days.

St. Mary's Church: A small beautiful island off Kochi is the venue of this church believed to have been built by the Portuguese in 1676. A week long feast known as 'Vallarpadath Amma' is held annually.

Kadamattam Church: 35 km from Ernakulam, this church is famous for its priest 'Kadamattath Kathanar'. Two feasts are held annually.

St. Thomas Shrine: This Shrine of Malayattur is situated at an altitude of 20,000 ft. It is believed to be one of the seven churches established by St. Thomas.

Kanjiramattam Mosque: It is situated 25 km from Ernakulam. It is believed to have been constructed over the mortal remains of Sheik Fariduddin. On the 14th of January every year, the festival Kodikuthu is celebrated.

Festivals

Among the Hindu festivals are the famous 'Sivarathri' celebrated at Siva shrines marked by 'Poojas and Prayers' and a number of customs and conventions, and another festival, 'The Arattu' which usually marks the conclusion of most of the festivals. There are also other festivals exclusive to the individual temples at various places. Vaikom Ashtami Festival is a grand celebration at the Mahadeva Temple.

At the St. Mary's Church, 'Vallarpadath Amma' is a week long ceremonial occasion to feast. It is an annual celebration.

Cochin Carnival Feast is observed during the last week of every year.

The Kanjiramattam Mosque celebrates the grand festival known as 'Kodikuthu' on the 14th of January every year.

Tourist Information Offices

- Tourist Information Officer, Dept. of Tourism ✆:91-484-2360502
- Govt. of India Tourist Office, Willingdon Island ✆:91-484-2668352/1913
- Airport Information Counter, Dept. of Tourism Kerala ✆ : 91-484-2611308
- DTPC Tourist Information Centre, Old Collectorate Bldg., Park Avenue ✆:91-484-2367334/2383988
- Tourist Desk, Main Boat Jetty ✆:91-484-2371761

Accommodation

Willington Island (STD: 0484)

- Taj Malabar (5 Star) ✆: 2668010
- Casino Hotel ✆: 2668221 Fax: 2668001 Email:casino@giasmd01.vsnl.net.in
- A T S Willington ✆: 2669223 Fax: 2667043
- Maruthi Tourist Home ✆: 2666365

Ernakulam (STD: 0484)

- Avenue Regent (4 Star) ✆: 2377977 Fax: 2370129 Email:avenue@md2.vsnl.net.in
- Bharath Hotel, P.O. Box No. 2357, Gandhi Square, Durbar Hall Road, Ernakulam, Cochin-682016. Email : bharathhotel@hotelskerala.com ✆: 91-484-2361415. Fax: 91-484-2364485
- Biju's Tourist Home ✆: 2381881
- Bolgatty Palace ✆: 2750500 Fax: 2354879 Email:bolgatty@md3.vsnl.net.in
- BTH Sarovaram, NH 47, Cochin Bypass, Maradu P.O., Ernakulam-682304. Email : sarovaram@hotelskerala.com ✆:91-484-2381881.
- Delight Tourist Resort ✆: 2228658
- Dwaraka Hotel ✆: 2352706
- Elite Hotel ✆: 2225733
- Gaanam Hotel Ltd. ✆: 2367123, Fax: 2354261
- Good Shepherd Tourist Home ✆: 2381154 Fax: 2352045
- Grace Hotel ✆: 2223584
- Grand Hotel, M.G. Road, Ernakulam, Cochin-682011. Email : grandhotel@hotelskerala.com ✆:91-484-2366283. Fax: 91-484-2364485
- Grand Tourist Home ✆: 2355206
- Hotel Abad Plaza, M.G. Road, Ernakulam, Cochin-682035 Email : abadplaza@hotelskerala.com ✆:91-484-2361636. Fax: 91-484-2364485
- Hotel Aiswarya, Near Jos Junction, Warriam Road, Ernakulam, Cochin-682016. Email : aiswaryacochin@hotelskerala.com ✆: 91-484-2381038. Fax: 91-484-2364485.
- Hotel Blue Diamond ✆: 2382116
- Hotel Crystal Palace ✆: 2352444
- Hotel Excellency, Nettipadam Road, Jos Junction, Ernakulam, Cochin-682016. Email : hotelexcellency@hotelskerala.com ✆:91-484-2378251. Fax: 91-484-2364485,2376901
- Hotel Grace ✆: 2353789
- Hotel Hakoba ✆: 2369839
- Hotel Joyland ✆: 23677664
- Hotel K K Intl ✆: 2366010
- Hotel Luciya ✆: 2380051 Fax: 2361524

- **Hotel Mayura Park** ✆: 2390560
- **Hotel Mercy** (4 Star) ✆: 2367379 Fax: 2351504
- **Hotel Orchid** ✆: 2319135
- **Hotel Rajmahal** ✆: 2371054 Fax: 2355377
- **Hotel Renaissances,** Palari-vattam, Ernakulam, Cochin-682025. Email : renaissances@ hotelskerala.com ✆: 91-484-2344463. Fax: 91-484-2364485
- **Hotel Rukmini,** Kalady Road, Angamaly-683573, Ernakulam. Email : rukminiangamaly @hotelskerala.com ✆: 91-484-2381038. Fax: 91-484-2364485
- **Hotel Sangeetha** ✆: 2367123 Fax: 2354261
- **Hotel Shaziya** ✆: 2376508
- **International Hotel (3 Star)** ✆: 2382091 Fax: 2373929 Email:international@vsnl.com
- **Maple Tourist Home** ✆: 2355156
- **Maruthi Tourist Home** ✆: 2666365
- **Matha Tourist Home** ✆: 2355221
- **Mundadan Tourist Home,** Angamaly-683572, Ernakulam Email : mundadancochin @hotelskerala.com ✆: 91-484-2381038. Fax: 91-484-2364485
- **Pamba Tourist Home** ✆: 2367111
- **Paulson Park Hotel** ✆: 2382179 Fax: 2370072 Email:paulson park@satyam.net.in
- **Pizza Lodge** ✆: 2364923
- **Quality Inn Presidency,** Paramara Road, Ernakulam, Cochin-682018. Email: presidency@ hotelskerala.com ✆: 91-484-2394040. Fax: 91-484-2364485
- **Queen's Residency** ✆: 2365775 Fax: 2352845
- **Queens Residency Hotels** ✆: 2365775
- **Sea Lord Hotel (3 Star)** ✆: 2382472 Fax: 2370135 Email:sealord@vsnl.com
- **Sun International** ✆: 2364162
- **Taj Residency,** Marine Drive, Ernakulam, Cochin-682011 Email : tajresid@hotelskerala. com ✆: 91-484-2371471. Fax: 91-484-2364485
- **The Avenue Regent** ✆: 2377977
- **The Best Western Viceroy** ✆: 2366477
- **The International Hotel,** P.B. No. 3563, M.G. Road, Ernakulam, Cochin-682035. Email: international@hotelskerala.com ✆:91-484-2380401. Fax: 91-484-2382091.
- **The Metropolitan (3 Star)** ✆: 2375412 Fax: 2375227 Email:metropol@md3.vsnl. net.in
- **The Woods Manor,** Woodlands Junction, M.G. Road, Ernakulam, Cochin-682011. Email: woodsmanor@hotelskerala.com ✆:91-484-2382055. Fax: 91-484-2382080
- **Udipi Ananda Bhavan** ✆: 2367641
- **Woodlands** ✆: 2382051 Fax: 2382080

Fort Kochi (STD: 0484)

- **Malabar House Residency** ✆: 2215083 Fax: 2221199
- **Fort Heritage** ✆: 2215333 Fax: 2225333
- **Hotel Fort House** ✆: 2221219
- **Hotel Seagull** ✆: 2217172

Wayanad

Facts and Figures

Area : 2,132 Sq.kms.
● Population : 786,627 (2001 census) ● Headquarters : Kalpetta ● Tourist Season: August to May.

It is bounded on the east by the Nilgiris and Mysore district of Tamilnadu and Karnataka respectively. On the north by Coorg district of Karnataka. On the south by Malappuram district and on the west by Kozhikode and Cannanore districts.

The name Wayanad is derived from the expression 'Wayalnadu' which means land of paddy fields. The Kabini river system of Wayanad is the perennial source of water to Cauvery.

This district seems to be second to none in its natural diversity of delightful landscape. The undulating region covered with thick verdant thick forests varies between 700 and 2100 m above sea level. With all the appropriate landscape and ideal environment, it is no wonder that the region accommodates some fascinating sanctuaries. The Banasura Project in this district hold an exclusive earth dam which will be the largest in India and the second largest in the world.

This is also the land of the tribals with the highest concentration of tribal population in Kerala. Tribal feasts, dances and conventions are still much in vogue here. There are a number of ancient temples, rock caves relating to the stoneage era, churches, mosques and antique monuments.

Air: The nearest Airport is at Karippur, Kozhikode, 95 kms from Kalpetta.

In and Around Mananthavady

Kalpetta: It is the headquarters of Wayanad district. The famous Ananthanathaswami Jain Temple is situated at Puliyarmala near Kalpetta.

Bhagavathy Temple: Situated at Valliyurkavu, about 3 km from Mananthavady the place is known for two temples. An annual festival for 14 days is celebrated here. Tribal dances and tribal feasts add nostalgic charm to the celebrations.

Erulam Sita Devi Temple: Situated at Pullapally about 8 km from Sulthan Bathery, the temple is dedicated to Goddess Sita the divine consort of Lord Rama in the sacred epic, 'The Ramayana' and their two Holy Sons Lava and Kusa. In the 2 day festival, Thira Utsavam, 'Theyyams' present ritual dances to invoke the deity.

Sri Maha Ganapathy Temple: Situated at Sulthan Bathery, this temple dedicated to Lord Maha Ganapathy, the God for successful initiation and thorough conduct of all events, celebrates an 8 day festival in which a variety of temple art forms takes place.

Sri Thirunelli Temple: About 30 km from Mananthavady, this temple also known as

'Sahayamalakshetra' is surrounded by beautiful thick forests. A two day festival is celebrated annually.

Kuruvadweep: About 17 km East of Mananthavady and 45 km Northwest of Sulthan Bathery is this 950 acre of gracious islands uninhabited and hence untarnished in its natural richness complimented by the serene river 'Kabini'. It is no wonder that the picnic makers are overwhelmed by the pleasant experience. This sylvan stretch is marked by orchids, herbs and birds. It is also known as Kurava islands.

Pazhassi Tomb: 32 km Northeast of Kalpetta, this tomb stands majestically as the memorial of 'Veera Pazhassi Raja' who is rightly remembered as 'The Lion of Kerala' who was instrumental in the famous 'Guerilla' warfare against the East India Company. The Pullapally cave gains historic importance since it was here the British captured 'Pazhassi Raja' at last.

The Glass Temple of Kottamunda: This temple about 20 km from Kalpetta, dedicated to Parswanatha Swamy, third Thirthankara of the Jain Faith has an interesting feature. The interior walls are fixed with mirrors in such an array that they reflect the icons of the Sanctum Sanctorum.

Pakshipathalam: About 10 km from Thirunelly, this is, as the name suggests, a centre for bird watching. The watch tower offers a better view of some rare species. Reaching the place on foot is the only means to get there.

Boys Town: This beautiful town is the outcome of the conscientious efforts of the Wayanad Social Service Society. It is 15 km north of Mananthavady. Nature Care Centre, Herbal Garden, Sericulture Unit, Permaculture Centres, etc., are the treasures of the town along with Jean Park, the Indo-Danish project for promoting herbal garden.

Chembra Peak: This is the highest peak in the district at 2100 m above sea level. It is an ideal place for trekking.

Banasura Project: About 25 km North-east of Kalpetta, this place 'Padinjarathara' is where the construction of the largest earth dam in India and the second largest in Asia. The magnificent site is also the venue of a fascinating sanctuary where perpetually blooming trees with their fabulous flowers add charm to the colour.

Begur Wildlife Sanctuary: About 20 km from Mananthavady this sanctuary is home to a variety of wildlife.

Edakkal Caves: 12 km from Sulthan Bathery, the two beautiful caves with their walls adorned with pictograph of the 'New Stonage' era, at an altitude of 1000m on Ambukutty near Ambalavayal bears testimony to the ancient civilisation that thrived here. Reaching the marvellous caves calls for a trek of about 1 km from Edakkal. Morning hours are ideal for a visit and the entry closes by 17:00 hrs.

Wayanad Wildlife Sanctuary: Abundant in flora and fauna the sanctuary with a variety of wildlife forms an integral part of the

Nilgiri Biosphere Reserve and in making inroads in the conservation of the regional biological heritage, the purpose it is intended for. It is adjacent to the protected area network of Nagarhole and Bandipur on the northeast and the Mudumalai of Tamil Nadu on the southwest. The life style of the tribals and others of the region have appropriately been taken into account by the management. Visitors to this sanctuary are required to obtain permisison from the Wildlife Warden, Muthanga Wildlife Sanctuary, Sulthan Bathery.

Nagarhole Wildlife Sanctuary: It is 40 km from Mananthavady. There are no bus services to Nagarhole from Mananthavady, only jeeps and trucks are available.

There is a PWD Rest House, Forest Rest House and Forest Inspection Bungalow at Mananthavady. The reservation authorities are the District Collector, Wayanad and the DFO, Mananthavady.

Brahmagiri: Brahmagiri, a trekker's paradise is a vast area of scenic wildland forming part of the Western Ghats. It is 11 km trek from Tirunelli. Brahmagiri lies 1600m above sea level. Pakshipathalam and Munimala are the other attractions. The Thirunelli Mahavishu temple, popularly called 'Thenkasi' or 'Dakshin Gaya' nestles in the lap of Brahmagiri.

Kuruva Island: 17 km east of Mananthavady and 45 km north west of Sultan Battery. But there are no good roads from Payyampalli. The best way is to trek 4 kms through the thick forest. There are six more such islands near the tributaries of the kabini river.

Lakkidi: About 5 km South of Vythiri, this calm and cool hill station, the gateway to Wayanad, at an altitude of about 700 m, forming a border to the Thamarasseri Ghat Pass is an enchanting place with looming peaks, splashing streams and thick forests.

Pooket Lake: This fresh water lake with natural intrinsic springs which never let it turn dry, in the backdrop of the sumptuous sylvan hills stands apart with boating facilities which offer thrill, a children's park where the little ones can be seen wallowing in their whims and a fresh water aquarium where the submarine creatures welcome the tourists.

Ambalavayal Heritage Museum: Just a little away from Ambukuty hill area, the museum tells tales of the tribe varieties of Kerala from their large collection of artefacts.

Chethalayam Waterfalls: This sensational waterfalls is located on the Pullapally Main Road, 12 km from Sulthan Bathery.

Panamaram: 29 km from Sulthan Bathery, this place holds the ruins of the once magnificent fort of Pazhassi Raja.

Festivals

A grand festival which runs for 14 days marked by tribal feasts and tribal dances is celebrated annually at the Bhagavathy Temple between February and March. The Thira Utsavam is a grand festival at the Sita Devi Temple. The Thomas Church and the Pallikkunnu Church come alive with grand celebrations in the months of January and February respectively. The Verambatta Mosque and the Mardoni Mosque have their festive occasions in the months of March and April every year.

Tourist Information Offices

* **District Tourism Promotion Council,** Kalpetta ✆: 91-4936-202134
* **Pookot** ✆: 91-4936-255207
* **Tourist Information Centre,** Collectorate ✆: 91-4936-204441
* **Govt. Guest House,** Sulthan Bathery ✆: 91-4936-220225

Accommodation

Sulthan Bathery (STD: 04936)
* **Dwaraka** ✆: 220358
* **The Resort** ✆: 220510-12 Fax: 220583

Kalpetta (STD: 04936)
* **Green Gate** ✆: 202001 Fax: 203975 **Email**:greengate@md3.vsnl.net.in
* **Haritha Giri** ✆: 202673

Mananthavady (STD: 04935)
* **Green Magic** ✆: 230437 Fax: 231407 **Email**:tourindia @vsnl.com
* **Elite** ✆: 04935-240236
* **Hakson** ✆: 240118 Fax: 240499
* **Reviera** ✆: 240322

Vythiri (STD: 04936)
* **Vythiri** ✆: 255366 Fax: 255368 Email: primeland@eth.net

Alappuzha

Facts and Figures

Area : 1,256 Sq.kms.
● Population : 2,105,349 (2001 census) ● Headquarters : Alappuzha ● Tourist Season: August to March.

This part as any other part of Kerala has a number of ancient temples with unique legends associated with them. There is also a temple dedicated to the 'Serpent King'. One of the churches here is believed to be one of the seven established by St. Thomas.

There are enough waterways to make the region fair and fertile. Paddy, Banana, Cassava, Yam etc., are among the sumptuous produce of the region. The exciting lagoons, the delightful dikes and the cultivation below the sea level all add to the astonishing elements of the region. The coir products of the region command a huge acclaim in the international markets. There are beautiful beach resorts, alluring amusement parks and exciting canoes. The ancient palaces bearing the evidence of a grand architecture and the museum with a variety of artefacts add to the greatness of the region. The town is popularly known as 'Venice of the East'.

The famous regatta is a special event here. The coveted Prime Minister's Trophy donated by the first Prime Minister of India, late Jawaharlal Nehru, attracts a large number of contestants.

Air: The nearest international airport is at Nedumbassery, Ernakulam, 86 km to the North. Trivandrum International Airport is 159 kms to the South.

Boat Services: Alappuzha is linked by boat service through the backwater to Quilon, Changanassery, Kottayam, Cochin, Kumarakom and Kavalam.

In and Around Alappuzha

Mullakkal Rajeswari Temple: This temple is located in the heart of the city. The Navarathri and the Thaipoosa festivals are famous here.

Sri Bhagavathy Temple: It is situated about 3 km from Alappuzha. A three day festival marked by traditional ritual folk forms like Kudiyattam, Padayani and Garudanthookkam is celebrated in a grand way.

Sri Mahadeva Temple: Situated, just 3 km from Alappuzha, this temple is dedicated to Lord Siva. The traditional art forms of Kerala, Ottamthullal, Kathakali, etc., are part and parcel of an eight day festival here.

Sri Karthyayani Temple: This temple is situated on the way to Alappuzha from Ernakulam at Shertallai. The roof of the sanctum-sanctorum is completely gold plated.

Sri Nagaraja Temple: Nestled in an vast expanse of verdant forests this temple is dedicated to Nagaraja, the serpent king. It is believed, by performing 'Uruhi Kamizhthal' which is placing a bell shaped vessel upside down as an oblation to the deity, childless couples are blessed with children. The sacred turmeric paste of the temple is believed to cure leprosy.

Gosalakrishna Temple: Situated on the Thiruvan Vandoor-Chengannur road, this temple is dedicated to 'Nakulan', the fourth of the five Pandava brothers of the legendary epic 'The Mahabaratha'. A 10 day festival is held every year. An exciting snake boat race is also conducted by the temple committee.

Bhagavathy Temple: At Chettikulangara, about 5 km from Kayamkulam, this temple has a huge oil lamp made of granite with more than 1000 wicks.

Sri Krishna Temple: Situated at Ambalappuzha, this temple is dedicated to Lord Krishna. A grand 10 day festival is celebrated annually. Sankaranarayana Utsavam, another 12 day festival is a musical time full of musical

concerts and soirees. 'Palpayasam', a sweet milk porridge is brewed during the festival. It was in this temple, the first Ottamthullal performance of the famous poet Kunjan Nambiar was staged in the 16th century.

St. George's Church: This church is located at Edathua, about 23 km from Alappuzha. An annual feast is held in April/May.

Kuttanadu: Regarded as the 'Rice Bowl of Kerala' this place

with its abundant paddy crops amazingly in the heart of the backwaters has to its credit the distinction of being the only region in the world where farming is carried out about 1.5 to 2 m below the sea level. This region with its intrinsic waterways strangely flowing above the land level with its sumptuous plantations of banana, Cassava and Yam leaves the visitors in sheer astonishment.

Alappuzha Beach: This beautiful beach is yet another crowdpuller in Alappuzha. The 137 year old pier can be seen here running right into the sea. The old lighthouse is also one of the attractions. The 'Vijaya Beach

Park' here offers copious amusement which includes boating facilities. The time and tariff of the park are as follows.

Visiting Hours : 15:00-20:00hrs.

Entrance Fees : Rs.2/- per head and free for children below 5 years.

Boating fees : Rs.10/- for 10 minutes.

Video Permit : Rs. 25/-

Camera Permit : Rs.5/-

Sea View Park: This is an ideal place for picnic makers. The beautiful park has a swimming pool and offers boating facilities too.

Boating fees : Rs.10/- per head, for 10 minutes on a 4 seater round boat.

Rs.15/- per head on a 2 seater pedal boat.

Rs.25/- per head on a 4 seater pedal boat.

Video Permit : Rs.50/-

Champakulam Church: This church dedicated to St.Mary and also one of the oldest churches in Kerala is believed to be one of the seven established by St.Thomas. On the 3rd Sunday of October every year, a grand feast is held. The feast of St. Joseph is celebrated on the 19th of March every year.

St. Sebastian's Church: Situated at Arthunkal about 22 km north of Alappuzha the church is an important pilgrim centre. 'Arthunkal Perunnal', the feast of St. Sebastian is held in January every year.

QST and R Block Kayal: If one wants to witness something similar to the famous dikes of Holland one should go to this place. The backwaters have been pushed back to reveal vast areas of land lined around by the beautiful dikes. Here farming and habitation about 4 to 10 ft. below sea level is a surprising reality. QST & R Block Kayals are accessible by boat from Alappuzha (1.30 hrs by motor boat and 30 minutes by speedboat.) Nearest Railway Station : Alappuzha Nearest Airport : Cochin International Airport about 85 km from Alappuzha.

Chavara Bhavan: Chavara Bhavan which is now a famous

pilgrim spot which receives thousands of devotees from far and wide was the ancestral home of the blessed Kuriakose Elias Chavara. The two and a half centuries old beacon here still retaining its original form can always be seen flanked by tourists. It is 6 km from Alappuzha. Boating is the only means to get there.

Krishnapuram Palace: About 47 km from Alappuzha at Karthikapalli this palace built by Marthanda Varma has murals dating back to 18th century depicting an episode from the Hindu Mythology, The 'Gajendra Moksham'. Apart from the exquisite murals which are the largest in Kerala, there are antique sculptures, ancient paintings and bronzes.

Karumadikuttan: The stately statue of Lord Buddha (made in black granite) dating back to the 11th century with a number of interesting legends attached to it makes the place a historically important one.

Nehru Trophy Boat Race: The not-to-be missed spectacle in Allappey is the Nehru Trophy Boat Race. It is a major event held on the second Saturday of every August and features the gigantic snake-boats of Kerala.

Competition is severe as the boats with over 100 rowers in each.

Festivals

A grand annual festival is celebrated at the unique 'Nagaraja Temple' here in October/ November. 'Chirappu' Mahotsavam is a big occasion at Mullackal Temple in December. Another festival celebrated by the temple is a one day Thaipooyakavadi. The famous Chandanakudam is celebrated at the Kidangamparampu Temple in December every year.

The churches here celebrate grand annual feasts, an occasion to regale and rejoice.

The 'Arthunkal Perunnal' is celebrated at the Jamma Masjid in Kakkazhom.

The famous regatta forms part of many festivals here at many places. A number of contestants are in the run for the famous Prime Minister's trophy, a trophy donated by the first Prime Minister of India late Jawaharlal Nehru.

Champakkulam 'Moolam Vallamkali': The traditional annual boat race of Kerala begin in July at Champakulam. This festival is known as 'Moolam Vallamkali'. 'Moolam' signifies Malayalam Nakshathram Moolam of the month 'Mithunam'.

Tourist Information Offices

* **District Tourism Promotion Council** ✆: 91- 477- 2253308/ 2251796. Fax : 2251720 Email:alp_dtpcalpy @sancharnet.in

* **Tourist Information Office,** Dept. of Tourism ✆: 91- 4772260722

Accommodation

Alappuzha (STD: 0477)

* **Marari Beach Resort (3 Star)** ✆: 2863801 Fax: 2863810 Email:casino@giasmd01.vsnl.net.in
* **Mankotta Island** ✆: 2212245
* **Kayaloram** ✆: 2232040 Fax: 2252918 Email:kayaloram @satyam.net.in
* **Coir Village Lake Resort** ✆: 2243462 Fax: 2241693 Email: coir@atdcalleppey.com
* **Alleppey Prince** ✆: 2243752 Fax: 2243758 Email: princehotel@ satyam.net.in
* **Palmgrove** ✆: 2245004 Fax: 2251138
* **Keraleeyam Ayurvedic Lake Resort** ✆: 2236950 Fax: 2251068 Email:mail@keraleeyam.com
* **Cherukara Nest** ✆: 2251509 Fax: 2243782 Email:zachs@md4. vsnl.net.in
* **The Green Palace Holiday Resort** ✆: 2726362 Fax: 2745351 Email:greenpalace@rediff.com
* **Padippura Residence** ✆: 2244978 Fax: 2243150 Email:babuncm@ md3.vsnl.net.in
* **Tharayil Tourist Home** ✆: 2236475
* **Sona Tourist Home** ✆: 2245211
* **Mutteal Holiday Home** ✆: 2242365 Fax: 2251961
* **Aditya Resort** ✆: 2244610 Email: sajipc@md3. vsnl.net.in
* **Hotel Komala** ✆: 2243631 Fax: 2243634
* **Arcadia Hotel** ✆: 2251354
* **Enkays Tourist Home** ✆: 2258462 Fax: 2802267
* **Santhatheeram Lake Resort** ✆: 0478-2582333
* **Kalpakavadi Inn** ✆: 2492239

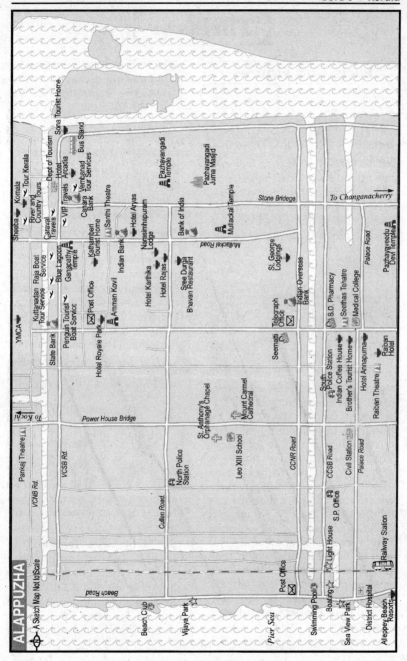

ALAPPUZHA

A Sketch Map Not to Scale

Thrissur

Facts and Figures

Area : 3,032 Sq.kms.
• Population : 2,975,440 (2001
census) • Headquarters :
Thrissur • Tourist Season:
September to March.

Thirusiva Perur which is regarded as the cultural capital of Kerala is situated in this region. The presiding deity of the temple of this place is Lord Siva. The

region is blessed with a number of temples whose architecture and sculpture would take us back by hundreds of years and a number of natural picturesque locations. The famous Guruvayur Temple is also located in this district. There are also ageold churches whose constructions and existence are landmarks in history. An ancient mosque much in conformity to Hindu temples in appearance can also be found in this region. The centre for learning traditional fine arts corroborates the rich heritage of the region. There are also museums of artefacts, art galleries and a zoo.

Besides the ancient monuments, the fascinating picnic spots like the dam, the waterfalls etc., add glitz to the glamour.

The Periyar, The Chalakudy, the Karuvannur and the Ponnani are the main river system in this district.

Air: The nearest international airport is at Nedumbassery, Ernakulam, 60 km South away.

In and Around Thrissur

Vadakkunnathan Temple: This temple is a classic example of the Kerala style of architecture. The temple contains the sacred shrines of Paramashiva, Parvathy, Sankaranarayana, Ganapathy, Sri Rama and Sri Krishna. Legend goes that this temple was founded by Parasurama. 'Thrissur Pooram' the

grandest temple pageantry in Kerala, is celebrated here in April-May every year.

Sri Maheswara Temple: The Siva idol in this temple was installed by Sri Narayana Guru, a social reformer and a rationalist.

Sri Koodal Manikyam Temple: About 10 km from the nearest railway station Irinjalakuda, this temple is dedicated to Lord Bharatha, Lord Rama's brother in the great Epic 'The Ramayana'. The eleven day grand annual festival marked by the enchanting pageant of 13 caparisoned elephants celebrated in April/May forms the conclusion of the festive season in the Temples of Kerala.

Guruvayur Temple: About 29 km west of Thrissur, Guruvayur also known as the 'Dwaraka of the South' is where this famous

temple dedicated to Lord Krishna is situated. A belief says that this temple was created by 'Guru' the preceptor of the vedas and 'Vayu' the lord of the winds. This is a popular pilgrim spot.

It is at this temple that Melpathur Narayana Battathiri composed his well-known Sanskrit devotional poem 'Narayaneeyam'.

Visiting 03.00 - 12.30 hrs and
Hours   : 16.30 - 21.15 hrs

Punnathoorkotta: There are over 40 temple elephants sheltered here. A number of tourists are overwhelmed at the sight of the magnificent beings.

Sri Kurumba Bhagavathy Temple: This temple at Kodungallur has access both from Thrissur and Kochi. The temple is dedicated to Goddess Bhagavathy who can be seen brandishing weapons and arms with all Her eight mighty hands keeping evil at bay.

Sri Ramaswamy Temple: Ideally situated on the banks of the enchanting river Triprayar, the temple dedicated to Lord Rama has episodes of the great epic, 'The Ramayanam' sculpted marvellously around the sanctum-sanctorum.

Mahadeva Temple: About 12 km away from Thrissur, this temple dedicated to Lord Siva is an architectural splendour of the traditional Kerala style. The temple complex spans a large area.

Puzhayannur Bhagavathy Temple: This Bhagavathy Temple which hosts a number of festivals is situated about 20 km from Ottapalam, a town near Thrissur.

Arattupuzha Temple: About 14 km from Thrissur, this temple is dedicated to Lord Ayyappa. The annual festival Pooram is a grand celebration in April and May during which the revered processions of the deities of 41 temples in the neighbourhood, to this village, take place.

Avittathur Siva Temple: About 4 km from Irinjalakuda this ancient Siva temple of architectural workmanship hosts an annual festival for 10 days.

Sri Rudhra Mahakali Temple: This temple is situated on the beautiful hills at Parthipara (Kavu-Vadakkanchery). The annual Pooram festival is a marvellous pomp and show here in April and May. Sparkling fireworks add to the colour.

Ariyannoor Temple: This temple at Kandanissery has a curved gabled entrance. The Siva

Temple at Thiruvanchikulam and the Sri Krishna Temple at Thirukulashekharapuram have resemblances to the 9th century architecture.

Archaeological Museum: Situated on the town-hall road this museum houses a variety of archaeological artefacts.

Visiting Hours : 10:00 - 17:00 hrs. Closed on Mondays and National Holidays.

Zoo: About 2 km from Thrissur, the zoo has a fascinating variety of wildlife and rare species.

Visiting Hours : 9:00 - 17:00 hrs. Closed on Mondays.

Art Museum: Within the periphery of the zoo, the Art Museum has an excellent collection of rare metal sculptures, wood carvings, ancient jewellery and so on.

Visiting Hours : 10:00 - 17:00 hrs. Closed on Mondays.

Town Hall: The picture gallery here is a treasure of mural paintings of all parts of Kerala. It offers an exciting experience.

Aquarium: The beautiful aquarium near Nehru Park housing a good variety of rare species is worth a visit.

Visiting Hours : 15:00-20:00 hrs.

Vilangankunnu: About 7 km from Thrissur, this piquant picnic spot is a picturesque hill which offers the visitors a nice, pleasant time.

Peechi Dam: About 20 km from Thrissur this beautiful dam site attracts several tourists. There are boating thrills to be experienced.

Cheruthuruthy: The world famous Kathakali Training Centre, the Kerala Kala- mandalam is situated here about 32 km north of

Thrissur. A number of art-fascinated young aspirants are taught and trained in the classical arts like, Kathakali, Mohiniyattam, Thullal, etc. The music and dance academy was founded by the famous poet Vallathol Narayana Menon.

Athirapally: About 63 km from Thrissur, this is a famous picnic spot at the entrance of the Sholayar ranges. The rolling and gurgling waters after an arduous climb down the mountains falling from a height of 80 ft. is a glorious sight to watch.

Vazhachal: 68 km from Thrissur, this sparkling waterfalls very close to thick verdant forests forms an indispensable part of the enchanting Chalakudy river.

Shakthan Thampuran Palace: Three tombs are visible from this palace which is also known by the name Thoppu Palace which spreads over a vast area of 6 acres.

St. Thomas Memorial: This old church at Kodungalloor which, according to a belief, is where St. Thomas landed, encompasses holy relics of the olden days. The church was obviously established by the Apostle. History cites the name of the place in 52 AD as Muziris.

Cheraman Juma Masjid: About 2 km from Kodungalloor town, this mosque, perhaps to bear testimony to religious harmony, has the appearance of a Hindu Temple. This temple-like mosque was built in 629 AD. This mosque stands apart as the first in India and only the second in the world where the Juma prayers were started.

Festivals

The 'Elephant Processions' are a great attraction in the festivals of the temples of the region. The Kodiyattam festival finds a grand way here. As in most parts of Kerala, 'Pooram' is celebrated with great enthusiasm. Exquisite boat races are also conducted which attract a large number of contestants and viewers.

Tourist Information Offices

- DTPC, Palace Road Chembukkavu ✆: 91- 487-2320800
- Guruvayur. ✆:91- 487-2550400

Accommodation

Thrissur (STD: 0487)
- Sidharth Regency ✆: 2424773 Fax: 2425116
- Casino Hotel ✆: 2424699 Fax: 2442037 Email: casino@md5. vsnl.net.in
- Luciya Palace ✆: 2424731 Fax: 2427290
- Manappuram ✆: 2440933 Fax: 2427692 Email: director@ mannapuramhotels.com
- Elite International ✆: 2421033 Fax: 2442057
- Alukkas Tourist Home ✆: 2424067 Fax: 2442003

- Yathri Niwas ✆: 2332333 Fax: 2371481
- National Tourist Home ✆: 2424543
- Central Hotel ✆: 2333314
- Hotel Peninsula ✆: 2335537
- Hotel Shalimar ✆: 2227744
- Hotel Merlin International ✆: 2385520 Fax: 2384962 Email: merlin@md3.vsnl.net.in

Athirapally (STD: 0480)
- Hotel Richmond Resorts ✆: 2769024
- Hotel Spring Valley ✆: 2764076
- Riverock Villas ✆: 0488-2834140 Fax: 0484-2374880 Email:riverokvillas@yahoo.com

Guruvayoor (STD: 0487)
- Hotel Sopanam Heritage ✆: 2555488 Fax: 2556753 Email:mail@sopanamguruvayoor .com
- Krishna Inn ✆: 2551723 Fax: 0487-2554169 Email: krishinn @md5.vsnl.net.in
- Vyshak International ✆: 2550964
- Vanamala Kusumam ✆: 2555213 Fax: 2555504
- Elite ✆: 2556215 Fax: 2555218 Email:elitechm@md4.vsnl.net.in
- Ayodhya ✆: 2556226
- RVK Tourist Home ✆: 2556226 Fax: 2554655
- Poornima ✆: 2556691
- Mangalya Tourist ✆: 2554061
- Sreekripa Tourist Home ✆: 2552415
- Nandanam(KTDC) ✆: 2556266 Fax: 2555513
- Hi-power Regency ✆: 2552296 Fax: 2556576
- Anjanam ✆: 2552408

Kannur

Facts and Figures

Area : 2,997 Sq.kms.
• Population : 2,412,365 (2001 census) • Headquarters : Kannur • Tourist Season: August to March.

The district is bounded in the east by the Western Ghats, in the west by the Arabian sea, in the north by the Kasaragod district and in the south by the Mahe region of the Union Territory of Pondicherry.

Going about the district, one finds no paucity of entertainment and enchantment, Kannur, formerly known as Cannanore is rich in ancient temples and monuments. The 16th century Portuguese fort, the Gundert Bungalow and a number of other monuments speak volumes of important historic events which had taken place in the region. The Mosque at Madayi Para was built of gleaming white marbles brought from Arabia, the birth place of Islam. An ancient Siva temple of the district, as alludes a belief, has references of having been in existence since two milleniums.

The region also has a plenty of picnic spots, beach resorts and hill stations. The wildlife sanctuary and the snake park of the district are much favoured by the enthusiastic tourists. The region also has a centre to teach and promote the cultural and traditional fine arts.

Air: The nearest airport is at Karipur, Kozhikode about 115 km south.

In and Around Kannur

Sri Sundareswara Swamy Temple: This temple is dedicated to Lord Siva. An annual festival is celebrated here attended by several devotees.

Sri Krishna Temple: This temple dedicated to Lord Krishna is located at Kadalayi about 6 km from Kannur. An eight day annual festival is celebrated here. Traditional art performances like the Kathakali, the Ottamthullal, etc., come alive during the festival.

Sri Jagannatha Temple: This temple located about 3 km from Thalassery is dedicated to Lord Siva. The deity was installed by the famous reformer Sri Narayana Guru. An eight day festival is celebrated every year.

Malliyottu Kurumba Bhagavathy Temple: This temple at Kunjimangalam, 4 km from Payyanur is dedicated to Goddess Kurumba. A five day annual festival is famous here.

Muchilottu Bhagavathy Temple: About 36 km from Kannur, this temple dedicated to Goddess Bhagavathy is situated at Kadanapally, Payyanur. The annual festival here lasts for 4 days.

Paralessery Temple: This temple is situated at Mundalur. The presiding deity is Lord

Muruga, the son of divine couple Lord Siva and Goddess Parvathy. An eight day annual festival is held here.

Sri Krishnaswamy Temple: This ancient temple which interests archaeologists and the layman alike is situated at Thrichambaram, 2 km from Thaliparamba. It is believed that the deity has been installed by Lord Parasurama.

Sri Annapoorneswari Temple: About 14 km from Kannur this is one of the temples where the grand Kerala architecture is at its best. The idols of Lord Krishna and Goddess Annapoorneswari are installed here. The annual festival here extends upto 14 days.

Kalarivathukkal Sri Bhagavathy Temple: Located at Chirakkal about 6 km from Kannur this temple is dedicated to Goddess Bhadrakali, the Goddess of 'Bravery'.

Payyambalam Beach: This beautiful beach is the favourite haunt of a number of visitors. It is situated about 2 km from

Kannur.

St. Angelo Fort: This wonderful fort on the seaside is a 16th century monument of the Portuguese. Francisco De Almeda, the first Portuguese Viceroy to India raised the fort in 1505 AD with the consent of Kolathiri Raja, the then ruler of the region. The fort had then been in the possession of the Portuguese, the Dutch and the British before it came under the canopy of the 'Archaeological Survey of India' lately. Mappila bay fishing harbour is an entertaining sight from the fort.

Visiting Hours : 09.00-18.00 hrs

Arakkal Kettu Museum: Arakkal Ali Rajas, the only Muslim rulers of Kerala had their residences here. It is about 3 km from Kannur.

Kizhunna Ezhara and Meenkunnu Beaches: About 11 and 12 kms from the town respectively, these beaches are most sought-after by tourists as well as locals for their beauty and solitude.

Parassinikadavu: About 16 km from Kannur this enchanting place is nourished by the serene 'Valapattanam River' on whose beautiful banks stands the famous Sri Muthappan Temple which makes the place a popular pilgrim centre. Boating facility and accommodations are available.

There is also an entertaining snake park nearby, with 3 snake pits, 15 glass cases and 2 glass houses exclusively for King Cobras. A fascinating variety of the reptile species can be seen here. Hourly snake shows are the 'Crown' to the endless entertainment.

Visiting Hours: 9:00-17:30 hrs.

Muzhapilangad Beach: About 8 km from Thalasseri and 15 km from Kannur, this elegant stretch

of about 4 km along the shallow waters, is probably the only drive-in beach in Kerala. Black rocks which forebode the deep currents, and clean waters are characteristic of this beautiful beach which is well suited for swimming.

Gundert Bungalow: 20 km from Kannur, near Thalassery, this mansion plays a significant role in the recent bibliography of 'Malayalam', the language of the State, since the first ever dictionary and a newspaper in the language were brought out from here. The great German missionary, scholar and lexicographer Dr. Herman Gundert had lived here for 20 years from 1839.

Valapattanam: It is about 7 km from Kannur town.

Attractions: The largest wood-based industry in South East Asia, a beautiful fishing harbour etc

Kannur is that part of the legendary Malabar Coast where King Solomon's ships anchored to

collect timber to build the 'Temple of the Lord' and to secure most needed spices. Here in the little hamlet on the banks of the river Valapattanam, is a giant of the modern timber industry - Western India Plywood Ltd., the largest wood-based industry in South East Asia.

The timber industry of Valapattanam thrive on the rich forest resources of the district. Teak, Iruli, Elavu, Karimurukku, sandalwood (Sandalum album) etc. are found in plenty in the forests here. In addition are cash crops like tea, coffee, rubber, tobacco, cashewnuts etc. Kannur is the only place in Kerala where *Pukayila* (tobacco) cultivation is carried on successfully.

Valapattanam is also a famous fishing harbour as well as the main source of the irrigation project in the district. It is a fascinating experience to watch the traditional mode of timber transportation - by tying long pieces of timber together and allowing them to float down the stream. Nearest Railway Station: Kannur. Nearest Airport: Karipur International Airport, Kozhikode, about 93 km from Kannur town.

Thalassery Fort: The construction of this grand fort, which served as the centre of military proceedings for the British, dates back to 1708 AD. The tourists to this place also have other attractions around; the Mosque, Jagannatha Temple; Sri Rama Temple and the Gym.

Visiting Hours : 10.00-17.00 hrs

Sri Ramaswamy Temple: This temple dedicated to Lord Rama, the divine Hero of the great Hindu epic 'The Ramayana', is adorned with marvellous carvings which are said to be 400 years old. This is one of the important ancient temples in Malabar situated in Thiruvangad, 23 km from Kannur.

Madayi Para: The wonderful mosque here built in the 12th century by Malik Ibn Dinar shines with white marbles imported from Arabia, the birth place of Islam. The Madayi Kavu Temple and Vadakunnu Temple add importance to the place. The ramshackle fort which had been a marvellous structure at Madayi is said to have been built by Tipu Sultan.

Malayala Kalagramam: The Kalagramam is at New Mahe, 29 km from Kannur. Painting, music,

dance, sculpture, etc., are taught here. This renowned centre craddles arts.

Thodeekulam Siva Temple: A prevalent belief relates the existence of this ancient Siva temple to over 2000 years ago. The Pazhassi Raja family is said to have had close associations with this temple. It is situated about 34 km southeast off Kannur and 2 km from Kannavam on the Thallassery-Mananthavady road.

Pazhassi Dam: About 37 km on the East of Kannur, this picturesque region with the beautiful 'Pazhassi Dam' draws flocks of tourists. The serene reservoir paves the way for added enjoyment, the pleasure boating. The project inspection bungalow and its dormitories provide accommodation to the tourists.

Ezhimala: This is an exciting spot, about 55 km from Kannur which couples the conjuring beauty of the elegant beach and the extravagant hill of about 286 m above the sea level. The hills here are treasures of rare medicinal herbs with amazing curative property. Carved stone pillars of ancient times sprout majestically from the ground at the hillfoot and an ancient burial chamber can also be seen. This is now a restricted area which can be entered only with permission since a 'Naval Academy' is underway.

Pythal Mala: This hill resort where tourists frequent and get delighted is about 4,500 ft. above the sea level. This region, near Kerala-Karnataka border abounds in flora and fauna. An interesting aspect is that it takes a trek of about 6 km on the challenging terrain to get to the top of the hills.

Aralam Wildlife Sanctuary: This fascinating sanctuary spreads over beautiful landscape of 55 sq. km. Elephants, bears, sambars, mouse deer and a number of other animals wander in their vast territories.

Kottiyoor: The beautiful river Bavali here flows by the ancient, famous temple dedicated to Lord Siva. During May/June a long festival which lasts for 27 days is celebrated every year.

Dharmadom: About 3 km from Thalassery lies the small island of Dharmadom. A bus ride from Thalassery will take one to the place of destination. The place was earlier known as Dharma-pattanam, getting its name from the popular belief that it was a Buddhist monastery as Buddha's images are said to have been excavated from this place.

Festivals

A number of festivals unique to the respective shrines according to the legends and conventions associated with them takes place. These festivals vary in nature, periodicity and the time-length over which they are celebrated. Some last for just a day or two while some others go on for 2 weeks or nearly a month. For instance, the annual festival at the Siva Temple Kottiyur extends for 27 days. Most of the festivals are aptly complimented by the traditional art performances.

Tourist Information Offices

* **District Tourism Promotion Council,** Near Civil Station, Kannur ℓ: 91-497-2706336
* **DTPC,** Tourist Information Centre, Railway Station ℓ: 91-497-2703121
* **Department of Tourism,** ℓ: 91-497-2702515, Email:info@dtpckannur.com

Accommodation

Kannur (STD: 0497)

* **Malabar Residency** ℓ: 2701654 Fax: 2765456 Email: malabar@sancharnet.in
* **Mascot Beach Resort** ℓ: 2708445 Fax: 2701102
* **Kamala International Tourist Hotel** ℓ: 2766910 Fax: 2701819
* **Costa Malabari** ℓ: 2371761
* **Hotel Palmgrove** ℓ: 2703182
* **Meredian Palace** ℓ: 2701676 Fax: 2701519
* **Safire Tourist Home** ℓ: 2760043
* **Hotel High Place** ℓ: 2700558 Fax: 2500344 Email: aquariusff@vsnl.com

PAZHASSIRAJA MUSEUM AND ART GALLERY
5 km from Kozhikode. On display here are copies of ancient murals, antique bronzes, old coins, megalithic monuments like dolmonoid cysts, umbrella stones etc.

Palakkad

Facts and Figures

Area : 4,480 Sq.kms.
• Population : 2,617,072 (2001 census) • Headquarters : Palakkad • Tourist Season: September to February.

The district headquarters, Palakkad town is situated on the Kerala-Tamil Nadu border where the combined influence of the cultures of both the States is largely felt. A number of ancient temples and grand festivals can be seen all over the district. The district has a long and rich cultural heritage. Traditional fine arts have flourished since time immemorial. The great names in classical music like Chembai Sri Vaidyanatha Bhagavathar and Palakkad Sri T.S. Mani Iyer hail from this district.

The entire region has a remarkable landscape with magnificent mountains in a lush green cover and enchanting rivers lending fertility to the land. There are a few beautiful dams of which 'The Malampuzha' and 'The Siruvani' are always in the limelight of any tour itinerary.

There are also numerous ancient monuments some still intact and some others though in ruins throw light upon the ancient people, their life style, the architecture, and so on and so forth. There are regions of reasonably thick tribal population. The wildlife sanctuary at Parambikulam, apart from hosting a number of the exciting species, also offers boating thrills. The ghat sections of the region are indeed too compelling for trekkers to resist.

Air: The nearest airport is Coimbatore, 55 km away. To the South is Nedumbassery Airport, 128 km away.

In and Around Palakkad

Loknayak J.P. Smrithivanam and Deer Park: (22 kms from Palghat) The Smrithivanam and Deer Park extended over an area of 100 acres of reserve forest at Walayar along the Kerala-Tamilnadu border. Deer and other animals move freely in this area. Facilities for elephant rides are also provided.

Thiruvalathoor: A 10 km drive from Palakkad, Thiruvalathoor is an ancient temple with some wood carvings and stone sculptures.

Meenvallam: The little known waterfalls at Meenvallam, 8 km from Thuppanad junction on the Palakkad-Manarkad route is a combination of enchanting beauty and scenic splendour. The water falls from nearly 20 to 25 feet and the depth is around 15 to 20 feet. There are 10 steps of waterfalls, of which, eight are located in the upper hills inside the dense forest thereby remaining inaccessible. One has to hire a jeep from Koomankund junction and then trek a distance of 1.5 km by crossing the Thuppanad river.

Punarjani Guha: Situated 2 km from the Tiruvilawamala Temple, the Punarjani Guha is a natural tunnel in the rocky cliff. Sri Raman is the temple's chief deity and the idol is believed to be 'swayambhoo' i.e. born on its own, and its abode is on the Western side.

Sri Vilwadrinatha Temple: About 15 km from Ottapalam, at 'Thiruvilvamala', this temple is dedicated to Lord Rama and Lord Lakshmana, the divine brothers in the great epic 'The Ramayana'.

Sri Thirumandam Kunnu Bhagavathy Temple: This temple dedicated to Goddess Bhagavathy is situated at Kongad about 20 km from Palakkad.

Alathur Temple Complex: This important temple complex at Alathur near Palakkad encompasses four temples dedicated to Lord Siva, Lord Krishna, Lord Varadaraja and Goddess Mahalakshmi.

Kottapuram Bhagavathy Temple: There is a temple dedicated to Goddess Bhagavathy at Kottapuram which is accessible from Palakkad.

Jain Temple: The place on the western outskirts of Palakkad town receives its name from the historic Jain Temple. 'Jainamedu', as the region around the beautiful 32 ft. long and 20 ft. wide temple is called, is where traces of Jainism having flourished in the region are explicit. The images of Jain Tirthankaras and Yakshinis can be seen in the temple.

Palakkad Fort: The beautiful old fort in the heart of the city was

built by Hyder Ali of Mysore in 1766. The British made some renovations and modifications in 1790. It is now under the protective canopy of the Archaeological Survey of India.

Fantasy Park: The amusement the park offers seems to make the fantasies come true.

Visiting Hours: 14:00 - 21:00 hrs. on weekdays 11:00 - 2100 hrs: on Saturdays, Sundays and National Holidays

Entrance Fees: Rs.30/- for adults and Rs.20/- for children. Pleasure rides and computer games carry extra charges.

Block Tickets: Rs.85/- for adults and Rs.70/- for children.

Pothundy: About 45 km from Palakkad, on the way to Nelliyam-pathy, the beautiful reservoir complex at Pothundy is the ideal place for short and sweet picnics.

Dhoni: This is a sumptuous sylvan region with a refreshing waterfalls. A three hour long trek has to be carried out to get to the foot of the beautiful Dhoni hills.

Malampuzha Dam: This exquisite dam and the conscientiously laid garden with a variety of brilliant and colourful flowers, the meticulously manicured grass lawn, the marvellous meadows, the fabulous fountains displaying an orchestrated water show, all that and a lot more leave the visitors spellbound.

The site lies in the cauldron formed by the western ghats. The gracious expanse of the serene lake formed by the dam provides boating facilities. The scenery of the numerous lights in a beautiful array breaking into the cool darkness of the night, like bright pearls arranged on a black sheet of cloth, is a breathtaking beauty. It is usually illuminated only in the week ends; however, it can be arranged on other days through the executive engineer on payment of a fixed fee. Adding to the fun and frolic are a swimming pool with high diving stages, an aquarium and pleasure rides like the boating and the ropeway winch and also a snake park and a children's park.

The garden opens by 10:00 hrs and closes by 18:00 hrs.

Boating : 10:00 - 18:00 hrs.
Swimming Pool : 12:00 - 20:00 hrs.
Aquariam : 13:00 - 21:00 hrs.
Snake Park : 08:00 - 18:00 hrs.
Winch : 10:00 - 13:00 hrs.
&14:30 - 20:00 hrs.
Pleasure Train : 08:00 - 20:00 hrs.
Telescope Tower : 10:00 - 17:00 hrs.

Kollengode: About 19 km south of Palakkad, Kollengode which literally means 'Abode of Blacksmiths' cherishes the rural beauty of Palakkad. The place also has ancient monuments like the Kollengode palace, the temple dedicated to Lord Vishnu and the memorial of the renowned poet P. Kunhiraman Nair.

Lakkidi: About 30 km from Palakkad, Killikkurissimangalam at Lakkidi has a historic monument which is preserved by the State Government today - the house of the 18th century poet 'Kunchan Nambiar' who is survived by his famous Satires and Thullal.

Meenkara: This beautiful dam across the enchanting river Gayathri which merges with Bharathapuzha is an exciting picnic spot.

Ottappalam: This town gains importance by the presence of several places of worship and a number of grand festivals during which the entire town swells in population.

Mangalam Dam: About 50 km from Palakkad the beautiful Cherukunnath river, a tributary of the glorious river Mangalam, is intercepted by the wonderful dam which makes it a popular picnic spot.

Thrithala: Ancient monuments and the dilapidated remains of the once-glorious structures signify the place. There is also a temple dedicated to Lord Siva and a ramshackle mud fort near the place. The Kattilmadam Temple, a small but subtle Buddhist monument (supposed to be of the 9th or the 10th century) made of granite on the Pattambi-Guruvayoor road, provides stuff for archaeological study. The Paakkanar memorial stands in honour of Pariah Saint near

Thrithala-Koottanad Road. This place is also the old sod of VT. Bhattathiripad, the famous writer and social reformer. This place is situated about 75 km from Palakkad.

Parambikulam Wildlife Sanctuary: Numerous wildlife creatures, the rare and the common, make themselves comfortable in the enchanting expanse of about 285 sq. km. The splendid reservoir amidst a picturesque environment makes boating and cruising possible. Accommodations are available at the rest houses of State Forest Department at Thoonakkadavu, Thellikkal and Anappady. For a tree house in the forest reserve of Thoonakkadavu, advance reservation has to be made. 'Kannimari', the famous, oldest teak tree is found here. The permission to visit the 'Sanctuary' can be obtained from, 'The Divisional Forest Officer, Parambikulam, Thoonakkadavu, Ph : 04253-277233

Siruvani Dam: About 48 km from Palakkad, the beautiful dam built across the serene river Siruvani is a popular picnic spot. One of the two gateways on either side of the length of the dam, is built in traditional Kerala style of architecture while the other in the traditional Tamil Nadu style. The region is also known for tribal population.

Nelliyampathy: About 467 to 1572 m above the sea level, 40 km south of Nenmara, this hill resort with its piquant evergreen forests spread lavishly along the incline and with vantage points which present to the viewer the diminished but spellbinding sight of almost a third of the distant, Pallakkad promises the tourists a memorable experience. Trekkers flock here to test their mites. For accommodation, contact the DTPC, Palakkad, Ph.: 2346212.

Chittur Gurumadam: Overseeing the benevolent river 'Sokanasini' which literally means 'Annihilator of Woes' is the memorial of Thunchath Ezhuthachan who authored the famous 'Adhyatma Ramayana'. The memorial houses a 'Srichakra' and some idols worshipped by the poet who spent his last days here. His wooden slippers and a stylus can also be seen.

Thenari: This place is famous for the temple dedicated to Lord Rama, the Hero in the great epic 'The Ramayana' and a natural spring in front of the temple. The waters of this spring is considered to be as sacred as that of the magnificent, perennial, Holy river Ganges in which a dip cleanses souls.

Mayiladumpara: Mayiladumpara which means, 'The rock on which peacock dances' abounds in the ever so beautiful bird, peacocks.

Attappady: About 38 km on the northeast of Mannarkad, Attappady is an awesome rendezvous of the magnificent natural elements like the picturesque mountains, elegant rivers and thick verdant forests. This is also the land of tribals which seems to keep the anthropologists busy. The Malleeswaram Peak which naturally resembles the Holy Sivalinga is revered and worshipped by the inhabitants. The 'Sivarathri' festival is celebrated with much enthusiasm. Accommodations are available at the PWD Rest House and a few private hotels at Agali.

Thiruvegappura Sankaranarayana Temple: The presiding deity of this temple is 'Sankaranarayana', a unique combination constituted on one half by Lord Siva and by Lord Vishnu on the other. This temple belongs to the 14th century whereas the auditorium here known as the 'Koothambalam' is believed to be a later addition in the 15th or the 16th century.

Ongallur Taliyil Siva Temple: This temple, near Pattambi, dedicated to Lord Siva displays the architectural skills of the period. Some of the most intricate laterite sculptures can be seen here. The 'Sivarathiri' festival is celebrated annually.

Silent Valley National Park: About 40 km on the northwest of Mannarkad, the once, seemingly boundless expanse of thick evergeen forests of the Sahya Ranges, now reduced to about 89.52 sq.km. has a salient feature which makes it known as the silent valley. The incessant chirping of the cicadas which is very common in sylvan regions is absent here. The beautiful river Kunthipuzha which forms a silver ornament to the valley before meeting the serene river Bharathapuzha, has its fount in the region which can be accessed. The visitors to the park must necessarily do a trekking of about 24 km since the ghat terrain makes vehicle movement possible only beyond that distance. The visitors have to obtain the permission of the Wildlife Warden, Silent Valley National Park, Mukkali, Ph. : 04924-2453225.

Festivals

Kalpathi Rathotsavam: This annual festival attended by a large number of devotees is celebrated at the 'Viswanatha Temple' in November every year. The temple Chariot Procession is the highlight of the festival.

Vela at Manappulli Kavu: This annual festival at the Bhagavathy temple is celebrated in March.

Kanniyarkali: This is an art form, patronised by the Nair Sect, which comes alive in the temples during March or April.

Nenmara Vallengy Vela: This is a grand annual festival celebrated at the Bhagavathy temple near Nenmara during February or March. Brilliant fireworks add to the holy mirth.

Pavakkoothu: This is a shadow play in the months of March/April at some Bhagavathy Temples.

Kaalapoottu: This is a thrilling race among the oxen used in agriculture. This usually falls in the month of January.

Konganpada: This is a ritual drama at the Bhagavathy temple in Chittur in the month of February/March.

Pattambi Nercha: This annual Muslim festival commemorates the Saint Aloor Valia Pookunjikoya Thangal.

Tourist Information Offices

- **DTPC,** Information Counter, Near Children's Park, Palakkad
  ✆:91-491-2538996
  Fax : 2530566

Accommodation

Malampuzha (STD: 0491)
- **Govardhana Holiday Village Resort** ✆: 2815264 Fax: 2815264
- **Garden House, KTDC** ✆: 2815217
- **Hotel Dam Palace** ✆: 2815237

Palakkad (STD: 0491)
- **Walayar Motels** ✆: 2566312 Fax: 2567162
- **Hotel Indraprastha (3 Star)** ✆: 2534641 Fax: 2539531 Email: eyepee@md3.vsnl.net.in

- **Kairali Ayurvedic Beach Resort** ✆: 222553 Fax: 04923-222732 Email:kairlpgt@md3.vsnl.net.in
- **Fort Palace Hotel** ✆: 2534621 Fax: 2534625
- **Hotel Rajadhani** ✆: 2521314 Fax: 2537317
- **Gazala Inn** ✆: 2546581
- **Merhaba Residency** ✆: 2525262 Fax: 2537833 Email:merhaba@eth.net
- **ATS Residency** ✆: 2537477 Fax: 2537037
- **East Fort Resort** ✆: 2532507 Fax: 2526977
- **Hotel Chanakya** ✆: 2537064
- **Hotel Ambady** ✆: 2531244
- **Surya Tourist Home** ✆: 2538338
- **KPM International Hotel** ✆: 2534601
- **Hotel Hilux** ✆: 2539433
- **Royal Tourist Home** ✆: 2535012
- **Hotel Devaprabha** ✆: 2823383
- **Ashok Tourist Home** ✆: 2536661

TALI TEMPLE
Situated in Kozhikode, it was built in the 14th century by Swamy Thirumulpad, a Zumorin. A remarkable feature of Kerala style architecture and a fine example of the total integration that can exist between wood and laterite.

Kasaragod

Facts and Figures

Area : 4,992 Sq.kms.
● Population : 1,203,342 (2001 census) ● Headquarters : Kasargod ● Tourist Season: August to March.

This extraordinary part of Kerala, with its scintillating natural features is aptly marked by a number of ancient temples and festivals. Measures are on to develop the city of Bekal into a fascinating centre of tourist attraction as it already has all the prerequisites to be one. The only 'Lake Temple' of Kerala belongs to Kasaragod. This region also has centres of arts and learning. There are picturesque hill resorts in the region on par with the famous Kodaikanal and Ooty of the neighbouring State, Tamil Nadu. The departments of 'Archaeology' and 'Agriculture' find interests in the region. The picnic spots here offer an assortment of amusement.

The region also has a long history of Islamic culture and influence. The Malik Deenar Mosque is of historic importance.

'Naturopathy', the natural way to the pink of health, has Nileswaram as one of its centres of renaissance.

Air: The nearest airport is at Mangalore, 50 km away. International airport at Nedumbassery, Ernakulam is 376 km South.

In and Around Kasaragod

The Bekal Fort: About 16 km on the south of Kasaragod stands the magnificent fort with its circular laterite structure about 130 ft. above sea level. This fort

overlooking the Arabian Sea was built 300 years ago. Just one kilometre from the fort is the beautiful 'Pallikere Beach' from where the fort is an overwhelming sight. The Aqua Park nearby has a variety of thrills to offer like the pedal boats, water cycles etc.

The Bekal Tourism Project is on its toes to make the naturally gifted place Bekal, one of the finest tourist centres.

Ananthapura Lake Temple: About 30 km from Bekal, this ancient temple amidst a serene lake belongs to the 9th century. The legend has it that this temple is the original abode, known as the 'Moolasthanam' of Sri Padmanabha Swamy, the presiding deity of the temple at Thiru-vananthapuram.

Kappil Beach: About 6 km from Beka Fort this beautiful beach, apparently isolated, offers calm and charm. The Kodi cliff at a stone's throw, is the vantage point to get an areal glimpse of the great expanse of the Arabian Sea.

Anandasram: This tranquil place is about 15 km from Bekal. Founded by Swamy Ramdas whose spiritual aura attracted disciples and followers from India and abroad this is an ideal place for meditation and spiritual endeavours.

Valiyaparamba: This beautiful backwater resort studded with picturesque little islands, greeted by four resplendent rivers attracts a number of visitors. The resort which also offers pleasure boating is only about 30 km from Bekal.

Manjeswaram: Sanctified by several centres of worship, the place also has a high yield of the cash crop 'cashew'. The two beautiful Jain temples here are situated on the banks of the enchanting river Manjeswar. The century old Gothic styled Roman Catholic Church, known as the Mother Dolorus Church is about 11 km from Kumbla. The oldest church in the district, here, 'Our Lady of Sorrows Church' was built in 1890. Manjeswaram also has the memorial of Govinda Pai, the forerunner in Kannada literature.

Kanwatheertha Beach: This is the favourite hangout of many. The natural extension of the waters in a calm pool like formation is ideally suited for swimming.

Kanhangad Fort: Also known as Hosdurg fort, this enthralling chain of forts suggests Somashekara Nayak of the Ikkery royal dynasty should have been on a fort building spree. The 'Nithyanandasram' here

is a tranquil spiritual centre of international recognition.

Sri Mahalingeswara Temple: At Adoor, about 45 km from Kasaragod, this ancient temple dedicated to Lord Siva has a transliterated inscription of Sanskrit in Kannada which is related to the Western Chalukya King Kirthivarman II of 745-755 AD. The environs of the temple are enchanting sylvan region which also has a rejuvenating river, 'The Payaswini'.

Cheruvathur: This popular picnic spot holds the ruins of the 18th century Dutch Fort in its beautiful Veeramala hills. The place has produced famous poets and scholars.

Kottancherry: About 30 km northeast of Kanhangad, this place with its picturesque undulating landscape, mountains and hills is a trekkers' paradise.

Chandragiri Fort: This beautiful fort of the 17th century forms an integral part of the chain of

magnificent forts built by Sivappa Naik of Bedanore. The fort is the ideal place to admire the glorious Sunset, the enchanting river and the endless Arabian Sea. There is a temple nearby in which the festival 'Pattu Utsavam' is famous.

There is also a mosque. The picturesque islands and inviting palmgroves nearby are piquant spots for the boat cruise. The Chandragiri bridge forms the boat jetty.

Ranipuram: About 85 km from Kasaragod and about 750 m above sea level, Ranipuram comprises an assortment of exclusive landscapes, the evergreen forests, monsoon forests, tall grass lands, pasture lands etc. The vast forests of Madathumala, the earlier name of the place, are contiguous to the forests of Karnataka. Mighty elephants grace the region. DTPC offers accommodation.

Madhur Temple: About 8 km north of Kasaragod, the wonderful temple known as 'Srimad Anantheswara Vinayaka Temple' is rich in its splendid architecture. The roof of the temple is elegantly copper plated. The temple is ideally situated in the pleasant environs of the beautiful river 'Madhuvahini'.

Edneer Mutt: About 10 km northeast of Kasaragod, the Mutt follows the 'Sankaracharya' tradition, an ancient tradition which has been in vogue since the period of 'Adi Sankara' the great religious reformer. This is also the renowned centre of arts and learning.

Possadigumpe: About 18 km on the east of Mangalpady, this picturesque hillock rising to a height of about 1060 ft. above sea level is a much sought-after spot for picnic.

Thulur Vanam: The temple here, about 4 km on the east of Panathur, is dedicated to 'Kshetrapalan and Bhagavathy'. This place also called 'Kekulom' is the venue of a grand 8 day festival led by the famous 'Sivarathri' which is attended by a large number of devotees.

Central Plantation Crops and Research Institute: This institute, abbreviated as CPCRI, established in 1970 has its headquarters in Kudlu, 5 km north of Kasaragod. Among its major activities are improving the genetic potential of plantation crops, production of superior planting materials, conducting research in various agrarian aspects.

Pandiyan Kallu: This rock sprouting from the sea, about 2 km from Trikkanad Temple, derives its name from the popular legend which says this rock was once a ship which was converted into a rock when one of the Pandiya Kings to whom the ship belonged, launched an attack from it, on the Trikkanad Temple. Now, this rock serves as the target of many an adventurous swimmer.

Malik Deenar Mosque: This historic mosque, the Jumma Masjid is believed to have been built by Malik Ibn Dinar. It is rich in Kerala style of architecture and is located in Thalankara, Kasaragod is revered as the west coast centre of Islam.

Madiyankulam Durga Temple: This temple dedicated to Bhadrakali, the Goddess for Bravery, hosts two grand annual festivals, one in May and June and the other in December and January. 'Bootham' a famous form of dance is the highlight of the festival.

Nileswaram: This town, regarded as the cultural centre of the district, has plenty of temples and festivals. The Kavil Bhavan Yoga and Cultural Centre here is famous for its 'Naturopathy' treatments and rejuvenation therapies. Nileswaram is also the folklore centre of the Archaeological Department. In the past, it was the home town of the great Nileswar Rajas.

Festivals

Pattutsavam: This 9 day annual festival marked by cultural performances, conventions and elephant processions falls in January every year.

Chaliyaporattu: This grand festival celebrated annually at Bhagavathy Temple occurs in March.

Palakunnu Bharani: This celebration is highlighted by grand processions and sparkling fireworks usually in the first week of March.

Nileswar Poorakali: This exciting event, usually from the last week of March to the first week of April at Bhagavathy Temples is a grand folk dance of men.

Palakunnu: This festival is marked by long processions of women carrying earthen pots which are then deposited at the local temple.

There are also other festivals celebrated with much fervour at homes and at temples. Traditional art performances form an indispensable part of most of the celebrations.

Tourist Information Office

* **Bekal Resorts Development Corporation Ltd.,** ✆: 91-467-2272007 Project Office Thanal Vishrama Kendram Bekal Fort ✆ : 9 1 - 4 6 7 - 2 2 3 6 5 8 0 Email:brdc@ sancharnet.in www.bekal.org

Accommodation

Kasaragod (STD: 04994)
* **Government Guest House** ✆: 230876 Fax: 230060
* **PWD Guest House** ✆: 230606
* **Apsara Regency** ✆: 220424
* **Hotel City Tower** ✆: 230562 Email:citytower @satyam.net.in
* **Enay Tourist Home** ✆: 2421164/ 2464

Bekal
* **Fort Land Tourist Home** ✆: 2736600 Fax: 2737471

Kanhangad (STD: 04997)
* **Elite Tourist Home** ✆: 2702276
* **Green Land** ✆: 2707203

SITE FOCUS

THE MATSYA KANYAKA
Thiruvananthapuram
Shanghumukham Beach, 8 km from the city nearer to the Airport. A gigantic, 35 m long sculpture of a mermaid.

THE NAPIER MUSEUM
Thiruvananthapuram
Built in 19th century, the Indo-saracenic structure boasts a "natural" air-conditioning system.

BACKWATERS OF KERALA
Kerala's centuries-old, palm fringed backwaters stretch over 1900 kms.

MALAMPUZHA GARDEN
10 km from Palakkad, a famous picnic spot with a dam.

Train Timings

The days of operations given within brackets below the Train Nos., the Arrival and Departure correspond to the **RESPECTIVE** stations.
All the trains are express trains unless otherwise mentioned.

Abbreviations

1) Alp - Allappuzha	26) Klm - Kollam (Quilon)
2) B.H. - Brief Halt	27) Knk - Kanniyakumari
3) Bkn - Bikner	28) Knr - Kannur
4) Bkr - Bokaro Steel City	29) Koz - Kozhikode
5) Blp - Bilaspur	30) Kvi - Kochuveli
6) Blr - Bangalore	31) LmT - Lokmanya Tilak
7) Brn - Barauni	32) Mdu - Madurai
8) Chn - Chennai	33) Mmb - Mumbai
9) Dbd - Dhanbad	34) Mng - Mangalore
10) Del - Delhi	35) Ngc - Nagercoil
11) Enk - Ernakulam	36) Ngr - Nagore
12) Gkp - Gorakhpur	37) NS - Non-Stop
13) Gnd - Ghandhidham	38) Okh - Okha
14) Grv - Guruvayur	39) Pal - Palakkad
15) Gwt - Guwahati	40) Pne - Pune
16) Hap - Hapa	41) Ptn - Patna
17) HNm - H.Nizamuddin	42) Rnt - Rajendra Nagar Terminus
18) Hwr - Howrah	43) Rjk - Rajkot
19) Hyd - Hyderabad	44) Shn - Shoranur
20) Inr - Indore	45) Tnv - Tirunelveli
21) Jdp - Jodhpur	46) Trc - Tiruchi
22) Jmt - Jammu Tawi	47) Tvm - Thiruvananthapuram
23) Jpr - Jaipur	48) Var - Varanasi
24) Kch - Kochi	49) Ver - Veraval
25) Kgq - Kasargod	50) Ypr - Yesvantpur

*6307 will be started from Ernakulam Junction on Thurdays and Saturdays.
*6308 will terminate at Ernakulam Junction on Thursdays and Saturdays.

Train No.	Train Name	Arr.	Dep.	Train No.	Train Name	Arr.	Dep.
				Thiruvananthapuram			
2075 (Daily)	Koz - Tvm (Jan Shatabdi)	20.55	-	2432 (Tu,Th,F)	HNm - Tvm (Rajdhani)	05.40	-
2076 (Daily)	Tvm - Koz (Jan Shatabdi)	-	06.00	2623 (Daily)	Chn - Tvm (Mail)	11.20	-
2431 (Tu,Th,F)	Tvm - HNm (Rajdhani)	-	19.15	2624 (Daily)	Tvm - Chn (Chennai Mail)	-	14.30

Train No.	Train Name	Arr.	Dep.	Train No.	Train Name	Arr.	Dep.
2625 (Daily)	Tvm - Del (Kerala Exp.)	-	11.15	6327 (F, M)	Krba - Tvm	17.50	-
2626 (Daily)	Del - Tvm (Kerala Exp.)	14.35	-	6328 (M, Th)	Tvm - Krba	-	05.30
2643 (Tu)	Tvm-HNm (Nizamuddin Exp)	-	14.20	6331 (W)	Mmb - Tvm (CST)	04.00	-
2644 (Fri)	HNm - Tvm (Swarna Jayanthy)	11.10	-	6332 (Sa)	Tvm - Mmb (CST)	-	04.15
6123 (Daily)	Chn - Tvm (Ananthapuri)	11.35	-	6333 (Sa)	Ver - Tvm	03.10	-
6124 (Daily)	Tvm - Chn (Ananthapuri)	-	16.20	6334 (M)	Tvm - Ver	-	15.15
6127 (Daily)	Chn - Grv (MS - Guruvayur)	06.40	07.50	6335 (Su)	Gnd - Ngc (Nagercoil Exp)	03.00	03.10
6128 (Daily)	Grv - Chn	21.15	20.50	6336 (Tu)	Ngc - Gnd	15.05	15.15
6301 (Daily)	Shn - Tvm (Venad)	22.10	-	6341 (Daily)	Enk Jn - Tvm (Trivndram Exp)	10.05	-
6302 (Daily)	Tvm - Shn (Venad)	-	05.00	6342 (Daily)	Tvm - Enk Jn (Ernakulam Exp)	-	17.25
6303 (Daily)	Enk Jn - Tvm (Vanchinad)	09.40	-	6343 (Daily)	Tvm - Pal (Amritha)	-	23.00
6304 (Daily)	Tvm - Enk Jn (Vanchinad)	-	17.40	6344 (Daily)	Pal - Tvm (Amritha)	06.05	-
6311 (Tu)	Bkn - Kvi (Bikaner)	03.10	-	6345 (Daily)	LmT - Tvm (Netravati)	18.40	-
6312 (Sa)	Kvi - Bkn (Bikaner)	-	15.15	6346 (Daily)	Tvm - LmT (Netravati)	-	09.50
6317 (F)	Knk - Jmt (Himsagar)	15.55	16.05	6347 (Daily)	Tvm - Mgr	-	20.45
6318 (Th)	Jmt - Knk (Himsagar)	19.15	19.30	6348 (Daily)	Mgr - Tvm (Bangalore Exp)	05.05	-
6321 (F)	Blr - Tvm	12.00	-	6525 (Daily)	Knk - Blr (Kanyakumari Exp)	12.45	12.55
6322 (W)	Tvm - Blr	-	16.05	6526 (Daily)	Blr - Knk	15.05	15.15
6323 (Th, Sa)	Tvm - Hwr (Shalimar Exp)	-	16.35	6603 (Daily)	Mng - Tvm (Maveli)	07.15	-
6324 (Tu, Th)	Hwr - Tvm (SHM - TVC Exp)	22.30	-	6604 (Daily)	Tvm - Mng (Maveli)	-	19.25
6325 (W)	Inr - Tvm (Ahilyanagari)	17.50	-	6649 (Daily)	Mgn - Tvm (Parasuram)	18.30	-
6326 (Sa)	Tvm - Inr (Ahilyanagari)	-	05.30	6650 (Daily)	Tvm - Mgn (Parasuram)	-	06.30

Train No.	Train Name	Arr.	Dep.	Train No.	Train Name	Arr.	Dep.
7229 (Daily)	Tvm – Hyd (Sabari Exp)	–	07.15	7230 (Daily)	Hyd – Tvm (Sabari Exp)	18.55	–

Kottayam

Train No.	Train Name	Arr.	Dep.	Train No.	Train Name	Arr.	Dep.
2623 (Daily)	Chn - Tvm (Mail)	07.35	07.40	6333 (Sa)	Ver - Tvm (Veraval Exp)	23.35	23.40
2624 (Daily)	Tvm - Chn (Mail)	17.30	17.35	6334 (M)	Tvm - Ver (Veraval Exp)	18.20	18.25
2625 (Daily)	Tvm - Del (Kerala)	14.05	14.10	6335 (Sa)	Gnd - Ngc (Gandhidham Exp)	23.35	23.40
2626 (Daily)	Del - Tvm (Kerala)	11.00	11.05	6336 (Tu)	Ngc - Gnd	18.20	18.25
6301 (Daily)	Shn - Tvm (Venad)	18.27	18.30	6343 (Daily)	Tvm - Pal (Amritha)	02.00	02.05
6302 (Daily)	Tvm - Shn (Venad)	08.15	08.18	6344 (Daily)	Pal - Tvm (Amritha)	02.40	02.45
6303 (Daily)	Enk Jn - Tvm (Vanchinad)	06.07	06.10	6347 (Daily)	Tvm - Mgn (Mangalore Exp)	23.58	00.03
6304 (Daily)	Tvm - Enk Jn (Vanchinad)	20.47	20.50	6348 (Daily)	Mgn - Tvm (Mangalore Exp)	01.10	01.15
6311 (Tu)	Bkn - Kvi	23.35	23.40	6525 (Daily)	Knk - Blr (Bangalore Exp)	16.20	16.25
6312 (Sa)	Kvi - Bkn	18.20	18.25	6526 (Daily)	Blr - Knk (Kanyakumari Exp)	11.25	11.30
6317 (F)	Knk - Jmt (Himsagar)	19.05	19.10	6649 (Daily)	Mgn - Tvm (Parasuram)	14.50	14.53
6318 (Th)	Jmt - Knk (Himsagar)	15.35	15.40	6650 (Daily)	Tvm - Mgn (Parasuram)	09.35	09.40
6327 (M, F)	Krba - Tvm (Korba Exp)	14.15	14.20	7229 (Daily)	Tvm - Hyd (Sabari Exp)	10.15	10.20
6328 (M, Th)	Tvm - Krba (Korba Exp)	08.30	08.35	7230 (Daily)	Hyd - Tvm (Sabari Exp)	15.05	15.10

Kollam (Quilon)

Train No.	Train Name	Arr.	Dep.	Train No.	Train Name	Arr.	Dep.
2075 (Daily)	Koz - Tvm (Jan Shatabdi)	19.37	19.40	2626 (Daily)	Del - Tvm (Kerala)	13.00	13.05
2076 (Daily)	Tvm - Koz (Jan Shatabdi)	06.55	06.58	2643 (Tu)	Tvm - HNm (Nizamudin)	15.15	15.20
2623 (Daily)	Chn - Tvm (Mail)	09.55	10.00	2644 (Su)	HNm - Tvm (Swarna Jayanthi)	09.30	09.35
2624 (Daily)	Tvm - Chn (Mail)	15.30	15.35	6127 (Daily)	Chn - Grv (Guruvayur Exp)	00.55	01.00
2625 (Daily)	Tvm - Del (Kerala)	12.15	12.20	6128 (Daily)	Grv - Chn (Guruvayur Exp)	02.05	02.10

Train No.	Train Name	Arr.	Dep.	Train No.	Train Name	Arr.	Dep.
6301 (Daily)	Shn - Tvm (Venad)	20.32	20.35	6334 (M)	Tvm - Ver (Veraval Exp)	16.15	16.20
6302 (Daily)	Tvm - Shn (Venad)	06.15	06.18	6335 (Su)	Gnd - Ngc (Nagercoil Exp)	01.40	01.45
6303 (Daily)	Enk - Tvm (Vanchinad)	08.10	08.13	6336 (Tu)	Ngc - Gnd (Gandhidham Exp)	16.15	16.20
6304 (Daily)	Tvm - Enk (Vanchinad)	18.50	18.53	6341 (Daily)	Enk - Tvm (Trivandrum Exp)	08.37	08.40
6311 (F)	Bkn - Kvi	01.40	01.45	6342 (Daily)	Tvm - Enk (Trivandrum Exp)	18.27	18.30
6312 (Sa)	Kvi - Bkn (Bikaner)	16.15	16.20	6343 (Daily)	Tvm - Pal (Amritha)	00.02	00.07
6317 (F)	Knk - Jmt (Himsagar)	17.05	17.10	6344 (Daily)	Pal - Tvm (Amritha)	04.40	04.45
6318 (F)	Jmt - Knk (Himsagar)	17.40	17.45	6345 (Daily)	LmT - Tvm (Netravati)	17.10	17.15
6321 (Th)	Blr - Tvm (Trivandrum Exp)	10.05	10.10	6346 (Daily)	Tvm - LmT (Netravati)	10.55	11.00
6322 (W)	Tvm - Blr (Bangalore Exp)	17.05	17.10	6347 (Daily)	Tvm - Mgr	22.05	22.10
6323 (Th, Sa)	Tvm - Hwr (Shalimer Exp)	17.35	17.40	6348 (Daily)	Mgr - Tvm	03.25	03.30
6324 (Th, Tu)	Hwr - Tvm (ShmTvc Exp)	20.50	20.55	6525 (Daily)	Knk - Blr (Bangalore Exp)	14.10	14.15
6325 (W)	Inr - Tvm (Ahilyanagari)	16.25	16.30	6526 (Daily)	Blr - Knk (Kanyakumari Exp)	13.35	13.40
6326 (Sa)	Tvm - Inr (Ahilyanagari)	06.30	06.35	6603 (Daily)	Mng - Tvm (Maveli)	05.35	05.40
6327 (F, M)	Krba - Tvm (Korba Exp)	16.25	16.30	6604 (Daily)	Tvm - Mng (Maveli)	20.25	20.30
6328 (M, Th)	Tvm - Krba (Korba Exp)	06.30	06.35	6649 (Daily)	Mgn - Tvm (Parasuram)	16.50	16.55
6331 (M)	Mmb - Tvm (CST)	02.30	02.35	6650 (Daily)	Tvm - Mgn (Parasuram)	07.30	07.35
6332 (Sa)	Tvm - Mmb (CST)	05.15	05.20	7229 (Daily)	Tvm - Hyd (Sabari Exp)	08.15	08.20
6333 (Su)	Ver - Tvm (Veraval Exp)	01.40	01.45	7230 (Daily)	Hyd - Tvm (Sabari Exp)	17.25	17.30

Kozhikode (Calicut)

Train No.	Train Name	Arr.	Dep.	Train No.	Train Name	Arr.	Dep.
1097 (Su)	Pne - Enk (Ernakulam Exp)	23.30	23.35	6333 (F)	Ver - Tvm (Veraval Exp)	17.50	17.55
1098 (Tu)	Enk - Pne (Poorna Exp)	03.25	03.30	6334 (Tu)	Tvm - Ver (Veraval Exp)	00.25	00.30
2075 (Daily)	Koz - Tvm (Jan Shatabdi Exp)	-	13.35	6335 (Sa)	Gnd - Ngc	17.50	17.55
2076 (Daily)	Tvm - Koz (Jan Shatabdi Exp)	13.05	-	6336 (Th)	Ngc - Gnd	00.25	00.30
2431 (Tu,Th,F)	Tvm - HNm (Rajdhani)	02.18	02.20	6337 (Tu, Su)	Okh - Enk Jn (Okha Exp)	17.50	17.55
2432 (W,Th,Su)	HNm - Tvm (Rajdhani)	21.43	21.45	6338 (Th, Sa)	Enk Jn - Okh (Okha Exp)	00.25	00.30
2601 (Daily)	Chn - Mng (Mangalore Mail)	07.45	07.50	6345 (Daily)	LmT - Tvm (Netravati)	09.15	09.20
2602 (Daily)	Mng - Chn (Chennai Mail)	17.30	17.35	6346 (Daily)	Tvm - LmT (Netravati)	19.05	19.10
2653 (Su)	Trc - Mng (TPJ MAQ Exp)	01.25	01.30	6347 (Daily)	Tvm - Mgr	06.10	06.15
2654 (M)	Mng - Trc Trichi Exp	00.25	00.30	6348 (Daily)	Mgr - Tvm	19.05	19.10
2685 (Expt. Tu)	Chn - Mng	04.15	04.20	6527 (Daily)	Ypr - Knr	07.10	07.15
2686 (Expt. M)	Mng - Chn	20.10	20.15	6528 (Daily)	Knr -Ypr	19.25	19.30
2977 (M)	Ern - Ajm (Maru Sagar Exp)	00.25	00.30	6603 (Daily)	Mng - Tvm (Maveli)	22.15	22.20
2978 (Sa)	Ajm - Ern (Maru Sagar Exp)	23.30	23.35	6604 (Daily)	Tvm - Mng (Maveli)	03.55	04.00
6305 (Daily)	Enk - Knr	10.50	10.55	6627 (Daily)	Chn - Mng (W.Coast)	00.05	00.10
6306 (Daily)	Knr - Enk	16.05	16.10	6628 (Daily)	Mng - Chn (W.Coast)	01.55	02.00
6307 (Expt.Th,Sa)	Alp - Knr	21.05	21.10	6649 (Daily)	Mng - Tvm (Parasuram)	18.40	08.45
6308 (Daily)	Knr - Alp	06.40	06.45	6650 (Daily)	Tvm - Mng (Parasuram)	15.40	15.45
6311 (Th)	Bku - Kvi	17.50	17.55	6687 (M)	Mng - Jmt (Navyug)	20.40	20.45
6312 (Su)	Kvi - Bkn (Bikaner)	00.25	00.30	6688 (Su)	Jmt - Mng (Navyug)	14.10	14.15

Train No.	Train Name	Arr.	Dep.	Train No.	Train Name	Arr.	Dep.
			Ernakulam Town				
1097 (M)	Pne - Enk (Ernakulam Exp)	03.55	03.57	6328 (M, Th)	Tvm - Krba (Korba Exp)	10.10	10.15
2623 (Daily)	Chn - Tvm (Mail)	06.15	06.25	6333 (F)	Ver - Tvm	22.25	22.30
2624 (Daily)	Tvm - Chn (Mail)	19.05	19.15	6334 (M)	Tvm - Ver	19.55	20.00
6041 (Daily)	Chn - Alp	08.35	08.37	6335 (Sa)	Gnd - Ngc	22.25	22.30
6042 (Daily)	Alp - Chn	17.30	17.32	6336 (Tu)	Ngc - Gnd	19.55	20.00
6127 (Daily)	Chn - Grv	03.57	03.59	6343 (Daily)	Tvm - Pal (Amritha)	03.25	03.30
6128 (Daily)	Grv - Chn	22.50	22.52	6344 (Daily)	Pal - Tvm (Amritha)	01.20	01.30
6301 (Daily)	Shn - Tvm (Venad)	16.23	16.25	6347 (Daily)	Tvm - Mng	01.25	01.30
6302 (Daily)	Tvm - Shn (Venad)	10.02	10.04	6348 (Daily)	Mng - Tvm	23.57	00.02
6306 (Daily)	Knr - Enk	19.59	20.00	6649 (Daily)	Mng - Tvm (Parasuram)	13.25	13.30
6307* (Expt.Th,Sa)	Alp - Knr	16.25	16.27	6650 (Daily)	Tvm - Mng (Parasuram)	11.05	11.10
6308* (Expt.Th,Sa)	Knr - Alp	11.08	11.10	6525 (Daily)	Knk - Blr	17.45	17.55
6311 (Th)	Bkn - Kvi	22.25	22.30	6526 (Daily)	Blr - Knk	10.00	10.10
6312 (Sa)	Kvi - Bkn (Bikaner)	19.55	20.00	6865 (Daily)	Trc - Enk Jn	05.08	05.10
6317 (F)	Knk - Jmt (Himsagar)	20.30	20.40	6866 (Daily)	Enk Jn - Trc	22.18	22.20
6318 (Th)	Jmt - Knk (Himsagar)	14.15	14.25	7229 (Daily)	Tvm - Hyd (Sabari Exp)	11.40	11.50
6327 (M, F)	Krba - Tvm	12.55	13.00	7230 (Daily)	Hyd - Tvm (Sabari Exp)	13.40	13.50
			Ernakulam Junction				
1097 (M)	Pne - Enk (Poorna)	04.20	-	2431 (Tu,Th,F)	Tvm - HNm (Rajdhani)	22.30	22.35
1098 (M)	Enk - Pne (Poorna)	-	23.20	2432 (Tu,Th,F)	HNm - Tvm (Rajdhani)	01.40	01.45
2075 (Daily)	Koz - Tvm (Jan Shatabdi)	17.20	17.25	2625 (Daily)	Tvm - Del (Kerala)	15.30	15.40
2076 (Daily)	Tvm - Koz (Jan Shatabdi)	09.15	09.20	2626 (Daily)	Del - Tvm (Kerala)	09.30	09.45

Train No.	Train Name	Arr.	Dep.	Train No.	Train Name	Arr.	Dep.
2643 (Tu)	Tvm- HNm (Nizamuthin Exp)	18.40	18.45	6310 (Sa,Su)	Ptn - Enk Jn	17.30	-
2644 (Su)	HNm - Tvm (Swarna Jayanthi Exp)	05.50	06.00	6321 (F)	Blr - Tvm (Trivandrum Exp)	06.20	06.30
2645 (Sa)	Enk Jn - HNm (Millennium)	-	18.45	6322 (W)	Tvm - Blr (Bangalore Exp)	20.25	20.35
2646 (Th)	HNm - Enk Jn (Millennium)	06.00	-	6323 (Th, Sa)	Tvm - Hwr (Shalimar Exp)	20.55	21.05
2683 (W, Su)	Enk Jn - Blr	-	17.00	6324 (Tu, Th)	Hwr - Tvm	17.25	17.35
2684 (M, Th)	Blr - Enk Jn	04.20	-	6325 (W)	Inr - Tvm (Ahilyanagari)	13.10	13.20
3351 (Daily)	Dbd - Alp	18.10	18.20	6326 (Sa)	Tvm - Inr (Ahilyanagari)	09.55	10.05
3352 (Daily)	Alp - Dbd	07.10	07.15	6331 (Tu)	Mmb - Tvm (CST)	23.35	23.45
6041 (Daily)	Chn - Alp	09.00	09.10	6332 (Sa)	Tvm - Mmb (CST)	08.20	08.30
6042 (Daily)	Alp - Chn	17.15	17.20	6337 (Tu,Su)	Okh - Enk Jn	22.50	-
6127 (Daily)	Chn - Grv	03.40	03.50	6338 (W,F)	Enk Jn - Okh	-	19.50
6128 (Daily)	Grv - Chn	23.05	23.15	6341 (Daily)	Enk Jn - Tvm	-	05.50
6301 (Daily)	Shn - Tvm (Venad)	16.45	17.00	6342 (Daily)	Tvm - Enk Jn	21.30	-
6302 (Daily)	Tvm - Shn (Venad)	09.45	09.55	6345 (Daily)	LmT - Tvm (Netravati)	16.20	16.22
6303 (Daily)	Enk Jn - Tvm (Vanchinad)	-	05.00	6346 (Daily)	Tvm - LmT (Netravati)	13.50	14.00
6304 (Daily)	Tvm - Enk Jn (Vanchinad)	22.20	-	6359 (Sa)	Enk - Rnt	-	22.45
6305 (Daily)	Enk - Knr	-	06.50	6360 (Sa)	Rnt - Enk	23.45	-
6306 (Daily)	Knr - Enk	20.25	-	6603 (Daily)	Mng - Tvm (Maveli)	02.25	02.35
6307* (Expt.Th, Sa)	Alp-Enk-Knr	16.15	16.20	6604 (Daily)	Tvm - Mng (Maveli)	23.25	23.35
6308* (Expt.Th, Sa)	Knr-Enk-Alp	11.25	11.30	6865 (Daily)	Trc - Enk Jn	05.40	-
6309 (M,Tu)	Enk Jn - Ptn	-	16.40	6866 (Daily)	Enk Jn - Trc	-	22.15

Train No.	Train Name	Arr.	Dep.	Train No.	Train Name	Arr.	Dep.
Alappuzha (Alleppey)							
2075 (Daily)	Koz - Tvm (Jan Shatabdi)	18.12	18.15	6322 (W)	Tvm - Blr	19.20	19.25
2076 (Daily)	Tvm - Koz (Jan Shatabdi)	08.13	08.15	6323 (Th, Sa)	Tvm - Hwr (Shalimar)	19.30	19.35
2643 (Tu)	Tvm - HNm	16.47	16.50	6324 (Su, Tu)	Hwr - Tvm	18.40	18.45
2644 (Su)	HNm - Tvm	07.17	07.20	6325 (W)	Inr - Tvm (Ahilyanagri Exp)	14.32	14.35
3351 (Daily)	Dbd - Alp	20.25	-	6326 (Sa)	Tvm - Inr (Ahilyanagri Exp)	08.02	08.05
3352 (Daily)	Alp - Dbd	-	06.00	6331 (M)	Mmb - Tvm (CST)	00.45	00.50
6041 (Daily)	Chn - Alp	10.50	-	6332 (Sa)	Tvm - Mmb (CST)	06.50	06.55
6042 (Daily)	Alp - Chn	-	16.00	6341 (Daily)	Enk Jn - Tvm (Trivandrum Exp)	06.57	07.00
6127 (Daily)	Chn - Grv	02.25	02.30	6342 (Daily)	Tvm - Enk Jn (Ernakumal Exp)	20.17	20.20
6128 (Daily)	Grv - Chn	00.10	00.13	6345 (Daily)	LmT - Tvm (Netravati)	15.25	15.30
6307* (Daily)	Alp-Enk-Knr	-	15.00	6346 (Daily)	Tvm - LmT (Netravati)	12.45	12.50
6308* (Daily)	Knr-Enk-Alp	12.55	-	6603 (Daily)	Mng - Tvm (Maveli)	03.40	03.45
6321 (F)	Blr - Tvm	07.50	07.53	6604 (Daily)	Tvm - Mng (Maveli)	21.55	22.00
Thrissur							
1097 (M)	Pne - Enk (Poorna)	02.20	02.25	2623 (Daily)	Chn - Tvm (Mail)	04.45	04.50
1098 (Tu)	Enk - Pne (Poorna)	00.45	00.50	2624 (Daily)	Tvm - Chn (Mail)	20.35	20.40
2075 (Daily)	Koz - Tvn	15.45	15.47	2625 (Daily)	Tvm - Del (Kerala)	17.10	17.15
2076 (Daily)	Tvm - Koz	10.32	10.34	2626 (Daily)	Del - Tvm (Kerala)	07.50	07.55
2431 (Tu,Th,F)	Tvm - HNm (Rajdhani)	23.52	23.55	2643 (Tu)	Tvm - HNm (Nizamudhin)	20.15	20.20
2432 (Th,F,Tu)	HNm - Tvm (Rajdhani)	00.10	00.13	2644 (Su)	HNm - Tvm (Nizamudhin)	04.00	04.05

Train No.	Train Name	Arr.	Dep.	Train No.	Train Name	Arr.	Dep.
2645 (Sa)	Enk - HNm (Millennium)	20.15	20.20	6321 (F)	Blr - Tvm (Trivandrum Exp)	04.35	04.40
2646 (Th)	HNm - Enk (Millennium)	04.00	04.05	6322 (W)	Tvm - Blr (Bangalore Exp)	22.00	22.05
2683 (W, Su)	Enk Jn - Blr	18.20	18.25	6323 (Th, Sa)	Tvm - Hwr (Shalimar Exp)	22.25	22.30
2684 (Tu, F)	Blr - Enk Jn	02.30	02.35	6324 (Th, Tu)	Hwr - Tvm	15.30	15.35
3351 (Daily)	Dbd - Alp	16.05	16.10	6325 (W)	Inr - Tvm (Ahilyanagari)	11.15	11.20
3352 (Daily)	Alp - Dbd	08.30	08.35	6326 (Sa)	Tvm - Inr (Ahilyanagari)	11.40	11.45
6041 (Daily)	Chn - Alp	06.55	07.00	6327 (M, F)	Krba - Tvm (Korba Exp)	11.15	11.20
6042 (Daily)	Alp - Chn	19.00	19.05	6328 (M, Th)	Tvm - Krba (Korba Exp)	11.40	11.45
6127 (Daily)	Chn - Grv	05.30	05.33	6331 (Tu)	Mmb - Tvm (CST)	21.45	21.50
6128 (Daily)	Grv - Chn	21.20	21.25	6332 (Sa)	Tvm - Mmb (CST)	09.55	10.00
6301 (Daily)	Shn - Tvm (Venad)	14.54	14.57	6333 (F)	Ver - Tvm (Veraval Exp)	20.50	20.55
6302 (Daily)	Tvm - Shn (Venad)	11.22	11.25	6334 (M)	Tvm - Ver (Veraval Exp)	21.20	21.25
6305 (Daily)	Enk - Knr	08.07	08.10	6335 (Sa)	Gnd - Ngc	20.50	20.55
6306 (Daily)	Knr - Enk	18.40	18.43	6336 (Th)	Ngc - Gnd	21.20	21.25
6307* (Expt.Th,Sa)	Alp-Enk-Knr	17.57	18.00	6337 (Tu,Su)	Okh - Enk Jn	20.50	20.55
6308* (Expt.Th,Sa)	Knr-Enk-Alp	09.35	09.38	6338 (W,F)	Enk Jn - Okh	21.20	21.25
6309 (Tu)	Enk Jn - Ptn	18.35	18.40	6343 (Daily)	Tvm - Pal (Amritha)	04.50	04.55
6310 (Su)	Ptn - Enk Jn	15.30	15.35	6344 (Daily)	Pal - Tvm (Amritha)	23.45	23.50
6311 (Th)	Bkn - Kvi (Bikaner Exp)	20.50	20.55	6345 (Daily)	LmT - Tvm (Netravati)	12.15	12.20
6312 (Sa)	Kvi - Bkn (Bikaner Exp)	21.20	22.25	6346 (Daily)	Tvm - LmT (Netravati)	15.35	15.40
6317 (F)	Knk - Jmt (Himsagar)	22.00	22.05	6347 (Daily)	Tvm - Mgr	03.00	03.05
6318 (Th)	Jmt - Knk (Himsagar)	12.50	12.55	6348 (Daily)	Mgr - Tvm	22.15	22.20

Train No.	Train Name	Arr.	Dep.	Train No.	Train Name	Arr.	Dep.
6359 (Su)	Ngc - Hwr (Gurudev)	00.15	00.20	6649 (Daily)	Mng - Tvm (Parasuram)	11.50	11.53
6360 (Th)	Rnt - Enk	21.45	21.50	6650 (Daily)	Tvm - Mng (Parasuram)	12.35	12.40
6525 (Daily)	Knk - Blr (Bangalore Exp)	19.40	19.45	6865 (Daily)	Trc - Ern Jn.	03.40	03.45
6526 (Daily)	Blr - Knk (Kanayakumari Exp)	08.10	08.15	6866 (Daily)	Enk Jn. - Trc	23.45	23.50
6603 (Sa)	Mng - Tvm (Maveli)	00.50	00.55	7229 (Daily)	Tvm - Hyd (Sabari)	13.10	13.15
6604 (Daily)	Tvm - Mng (Maveli)	00.55	01.00	7230 (Daily)	Hyd - Tvm (Sabari)	12.00	12.05

Kannur (Cannanore)

Train No.	Train Name	Arr.	Dep.	Train No.	Train Name	Arr.	Dep.
1097 (Su)	Pne - Enk (Poorna)	21.45	21.50	6307* (Expt.Th,Sa)	Alp-Enk-Knr	23.05	-
1098 (Tu)	Enk - Pne (Poorna)	05.10	05.15	6308* (Expt.Th,Sa)	Knr-Enk-Alp	-	05.00
2431 (W,F,Sa)	Tvm - HNm (Rajdhani)	03.45	03.47	6311 (F)	Bkn - Kvi	16.00	16.05
2432 (M,W,Th)	HNm - Tvm (Rajdhani)	20.08	20.10	6312 (Su)	Kvi - Bkn	02.10	02.15
2601 (Daily)	Chn - Mng (Mangalore Exp)	09.35	09.40	6333 (F)	Ver - Tvm (Veraval Exp)	16.00	16.05
2602 (Daily)	Mng - Chn (Chennai Mail)	15.45	15.50	6334 (Tu)	Tvm - Ver (Veraval Exp)	02.10	02.15
2653 (Su)	Trc - Mng (Tpj MAQ Exp)	02.55	03.00	6335 (Sa)	Gnd - Ngc	16.00	16.05
2654 (Su)	Mng - Trc (Trichy Exp)	22.50	22.55	6336 (W)	Ngc - Gnd	02.10	02.15
2685 (Expt.Tu)	Chn - Mng (Mangalore Mail)	06.10	06.15	6337 (Tu, Su)	Okh - Enk Jn	16.00	16.05
2686 (Expt.M)	Mng - Chn (Mangalore Mail)	18.20	18.25	6338 (Th,Sa)	Enk Jn - Okh	02.10	02.15
2977 (Su)	Ern - Ajm Maru Sagar Exp	02.10	02.15	6345 (Daily)	LmT - Tvm (Netravati)	07.25	07.30
2978 (Su)	Ajm - Ern Maru Sagar Exp	21.45	21.50	6346 (Daily)	Tvm - LmT (Netravati)	21.15	21.20
6305 (Daily)	Enk - Knr	12.45	-	6347 (Daily)	Tvm - Mng	08.10	08.15
6306 (Daily)	Knr - Enk	-	14.30	6348 (Daily)	Mng - Tvm	17.15	17.20

Train No.	Train Name	Arr.	Dep.	Train No.	Train Name	Arr.	Dep.
6527 (Daily)	Ypr - Knr	09.20	-	6628 (Daily)	Mng - Chn (West Coast)	00.05	00.10
6528 (Daily)	Knr -Ypr	-	17.45	6649 (Daily)	Mng - Tvm (Parasuram)	06.50	06.55
6603 (Daily)	Mng - Tvm (Maveli)	20.25	20.30	6650 (Daily)	Tvm - Mng (Parasuram)	17.35	17.40
6604 (Daily)	Tvm - Mng (Maveli)	05.50	05.55	6687 (M)	Mng - Jmt (Navyug)	18.45	18.50
6627 (Daily)	Chn - Mng (West Coast)	01.45	01.50	6688 (Su)	Jmt - Mng (Navyug)	16.05	16.10

Palakkad (Palghat)

Train No.	Train Name	Arr.	Dep.	Train No.	Train Name	Arr.	Dep.
2601 (Daily)	Chn - Mng (Mangalore Mail)	04.45	04.50	6041 (Daily)	Chn - Alp	05.25	05.30
2602 (Daily)	Mng - Chn	20.35	20.40	6042 (Daily)	Alp - Chn	20.55	21.00
2623 (Daily)	Chn - Tvm (Mail)	03.35	03.40	6309 (M,Tu)	Enk Jn - Ptn	20.10	20.15
2624 (Daily)	Tvm - Chn (Mail)	22.10	22.15	6310 (Sa,Su)	Ptn - Enk Jn	13.55	14.00
2625 (Daily)	Tvm - Del (Kerala)	18.40	18.45	6317 (F)	Knk - Jmt (Himsagar)	23.40	23.45
2626 (Daily)	Del - Tvm (Kerala)	06.30	06.35	6318 (Th)	Jmt - Knk (Himsagar)	11.10	11.15
2643 (Tu)	Tvm - HNm Nizamudhin	21.50	21.55	6321 (F)	Blr - Tvm (Trivandrum Exp)	03.25	03.30
2644 (Sa)	HNm - Tvm (Swarna Jayanthi)	02.40	02.45	6322 (W)	Tvm - Blr (Bangalore Exp)	23.40	23.45
2645 (Sa)	Enk - HNm (Millennium)	21.50	21.55	6323 (Th, Sa)	Tvm - Hwr	00.05	00.10
2646 (Th)	HNm - Enk (Millennium)	02.40	02.45	6324 (Tu, Th)	Hwr - Tvm	13.55	14.00
2653 (Su)	Trc - Mng (Tpj MAQ Exp)	23.05	23.10	6325 (W)	Inr - Tvm (Ahilyanagari)	09.10	09.15
2654 (Su)	Mng - Trc (Trichy Exp)	02.45	02.50	6326 (Sa)	Tvm - Inr (Ahilyanagari)	14.00	14.05
2683 (W,Su)	Enk Jn - Blr	19.55	20.00	6327 (M, F)	Krba - Tvm	09.10	09.15
2684 (Tu,F)	Blr - Enk Jn	01.00	01.05	6328 (M, Th)	Tvm - Krba	14.00	14.05
2685 (Daily)	Chn - Mng	01.20	01.25	6331 (Tu)	Mmb - Tvm (CST)	19.50	19.55
2686 (Daily)	Mng - Chn	23.00	23.05	6332 (Sa)	Tvm - Mmb (CST)	12.20	12.25
3351 (Daily)	Dbd - Alp	13.30	13.35	6343 (Daily)	Tvm - Pal (Amritha)	07.25	07.35
3352 (Daily)	Alp - Dbd	10.40	10.45				

Train No.	Train Name	Arr.	Dep.	Train No.	Train Name	Arr.	Dep.
6344 (Daily)	Pal - Tvm (Amritha)	22.08	22.10	6628 (Daily)	Mng - Chn (W.Coast)	05.05	05.10
6359 (Sa)	Enk - Rnt	01.45	01.50	6687 (M)	Mng - Jmt (Navyug)	23.40	23.45
6360 (Sa)	Rnt - Enk	19.55	20.00	6688 (Su)	Jmt - Mng (Navyug)	11.10	11.15
6525 (Daily)	Knk - Blr (Bangalore Exp)	21.35	21.40	6865 (Daily)	Trc - Enk	02.00	02.05
6526 (Daily)	Blr - Knk (Kanayakumari Exp)	06.45	06.50	6866 (Daily)	Enk - Trc	01.15	01.20
6527 (Daily)	Ypr - Knr	04.20	04.25	7229 (Daily)	Tvm - Hyd (Sabri Exp)	15.15	15.20
6528 (Daily)	Knr -Ypr	22.30	22.35	7230 (Daily)	Hyd - Tvm	09.55	10.00
6627 (Daily)	Chn - Mng (W.Coast)	21.10	21.15				

Kasaragod

Train No.	Train Name	Arr.	Dep.	Train No.	Train Name	Arr.	Dep.
1097 (Su)	Pne - Enk (Poorna)	20.03	20.05	6336 (F)	Ngc - Gnd	03.53	03.55
1098 (Tu)	Enk - Pne (Poorna)	06.39	06.40	6337 (Tu,Su)	Okh - Enk Jn	14.23	14.25
2601 (Daily)	Chn - Mng (Mangalore Mail)	11.09	11.10	6338 (Th,Sa)	Enk Jn - Okh	03.54	03.55
2602 (Daily)	Mng - Chn (Chennai Mail)	14.04	14.05	6345 (Daily)	LmT - Tvm (Netravati)	05.33	05.35
2653 (Su)	Trc - Mng (Tpj MAQ Exp)	04.14	04.15	6346 (Daily)	Tvm - LmT (Netravati)	22.54	22.55
2654 (Su)	Mng - Trc (Trichy Exp)	21.28	21.30	6347 (Daily)	Tvm - Mng	09.58	10.00
2685 (Expt.Tu)	Chn - Mng	07.54	07.55	6348 (Daily)	Mng - Tvm	15.20	15.22
2686 (Expt.M)	Mng - Chn	16.49	16.50	6603 (Daily)	Mng - Tvm (Maveli)	18.29	18.30
2977 (M)	Enk - Jpr (Marusagar Exp)	03.54	03.55	6604 (Daily)	Tvm - Mng (Maveli)	07.38	07.40
2978 (Sa)	Jpr - Enk (Marusagar Exp)	20.03	20.05	6627 (Daily)	Chn - Mng (West Coast)	03.18	03.20
6311 (F)	Bkn - Kvi (Bikaner Exp)	14.23	14.25	6628 (Daily)	Mng - Chn	22.18	22.20
6312 (Su)	Kvi - Bkn (Bikaner Exp)	03.54	03.55	6649 (Daily)	Mng - Tvm (Parasuram)	05.04	05.05
6333 (F)	Ver - Tvm (Veraval Exp)	14.23	14.25	6650 (Daily)	Tvm - Mng (Parasuram)	19.14	19.15
6334 (Tu)	Tvm - Ver (Veraval Exp)	03.54	03.55	6687 (M)	Mng - Jmt (Navyug)	17.09	17.10
6335 (Sa)	Gnd - Ngc	14.23	14.25	6688 (Su)	Jmt - Mng (Navyug)	17.23	17.25

Air connections

Thiruvananthapuram International Airport (Domestic flights ✆: 91-471-2316870, 2501542, Terminal : 2501269, 2500585)

- Domestic flights (direct): From/To: New Delhi, Mumbai, Bengalooru, Chennai

- International flights (direct): from/To: Colombo, Maldives, Dubai, Sharjah, Abu Dhabi, Muscat, Bahrain, Doha, Ras-al-Khaimah, Kuwait, Riyadh, Fujairah, Singapore

Kozhikode (Calicut) Airport,

(✆: 91-483-2711314, 2766669, 2767401)

- Domestic flights (direct): From/To: Mumbai.

- International flights (direct): from/To: Dubai, Abu Dhabi, Muscat, Kuwait & Sharjah.

Cochin International Airport, Nedumbassery

(✆: 91-484-2610070, 2649994, 2374154, 2610040, 2610050)

- Domestic flights (direct): From/To: Mumbai, Chennai, Goa, Agathi, Coimbatore, New Delhi, Goa, Hyderabad, Bengalooru, Trichy, Calicut.

- International flights (direct): from/To: Sharjah, Dubai, Abu Dhabi, Bahrain, Riyadh, Muscat, Kuwait, Dhahran.

Telephone Numbers : Thiruvananthapuram - Airport

Air India (Airport)	0471-2310310, 2315225
Indian Airlines (Airport)	2501537
Air India (Cargo)	2500585
Jet Airways	2328864
Jet Airways (Airport)	2500710, 2728864
Air Lanka	2460639
Air Lanka (Airport)	2501140
Oman Air	2328137
Oman Air (Airport)	2462987
Gulf Air	2327514
Gulf Air (Airport)	2501205/6
Kuwait Airways	2328651
Kuwait Airways (Airport)	2323436
Sri Lankan Airlines	2471810, 2471815
Sri Lankan Airlines (Airport)	2501140

Note : Please check with concerned authorities for prevalent telephone, fax numbers, tariff, train/air timings, etc.

SITE FOCUS

SABARIMALA
Dedicated to Lord Sree Ayyappa
One of the most famous pilgrim centres in India. 72 km from Pathanamthitta town. Pilgrim season: Nov. to mid Jan. every year.

ARANMULA BOAT RACE
Held on the last day of the week long Onam festival. The Partha Sarathi Temple here, on the banks of the holy river Pamba, attracts large crowds of devotees.

ST. ANGELO FORT
3 km from Kannur. This seafront laterite fort was constructed in 1505 AD by the first Portuguese Viceroy, Don Francisco De Almeda with the consent of the ruling Kolathiri Raja.

Lakshadweep

Facts and Figures

Area : 32 Sq.km. • Population :60,650 (2001 census) • Headquarters : Kavaratti Island • Tourist Season: October to May.

Lakshadweep means 'a hundred thousand islands' in Malayalam, the local language. However there are only 36 islands having a total area of 32 sq.kilometer. The Laccadives, Minicoy and Amindivi group of islands were constituted into a single territory in 1956 and it was renamed as Lakshadweep in 1973.

These islands lie scattered in the Arabian sea about 280-480 kms off Kerala coast. It is the tiniest Union Territory of India with 12 atolls, 3 reefs and 5 submerged banks. Eleven islands are inhabited.

The advent of Islam dates back to the 7th century. Ubaidulla

started propagating Islam in the islands. Still 93% of the inhabitants of Lakshadweep are Muslims.

People are mostly engaged in fishing and coconut cultivation.

The islands are virtually crime-free.

Food: Spiced coconut-rich Vegetarian & Non vegetarian food. Curried, fried and barbecued fish.

Tourist Season: October - May for the ship based tour packages. Agatti and Bangaram may be visited throughout the year.

Things not to do: Consumption of alcoholic beverages is prohibited in all islands except Bangaram. Picking up Corals is a punishable crime.

Tourism in Lakshadweep

Lakshadweep is one of the worlds most spectacular tropical island systems. Thirty-two sq.km of land spread over 36 islands surrounded by 4200 sq.km of lagoon rich in marine wealth. The precious heritage of ecology and culture is supported by an extremely fragile ecosystem. Union Territory of Lakshadweep has consciously followed a middle path between tourism promotion and environmental conservation. The Administration has taken steps to promote tourism in a way that is consistent with ecological concerns. As an effective strategy to avoid pressure on ecological environment, the efforts to promote tourism have been synchronized with the carrying capacity of the islands.

Though all the islands are endowed with the beauty of coral reef, sandy beaches, unpolluted and clear water and hospitable settings, most of these differ in terms of facilities and services offered. Some islands have been promoted for diving and water sports; still others have been developed so that people enjoy the charm of relaxation and natural enjoyment. Since the land is precious and scarce it is avowed policy of the Administration to relieve pressure on land and promote water based tourism. The motto being admires and not exploits that natural beauty.

The Lakshadweep administration has taken a holistic view of tourism development. It promotes tourism as a composite package, comprising accommodation, transportation from and / to main land by ship / air, catering facilities, recreational facilities, water sports, scuba diving, boating, wind surfing etc.The facilities in two islands ie. Bangaram and Agatti are being managed by private agencies. Private divers also run the scuba diving school at Kadmat. The thrust is on promoting ship based tourism for Indian nationals at affordable rates and the local Administration's efforts in the regard has met with great success. As the ship cannot enter the lagoon, the passengers are transferred on small boats and brought to the island jetty.

Sea: Four all weather ships M.V. Bharat seema, M.V. Tipu Sultan, M.V. Amindivi and M.V. Minicoy operate between Kochi and the islands. The passage takes between 14 to 20 hours.

Air: Indian Airlines operate

flight from Kochi to Agatti island every day except Sunday. The flight from Kochi to Agatti takes approximately one hour thirty minutes.

Kavaratti: Kavaratti, the most developed island is the head quarters of this Union Territory. This island is about 6 km in length and about 1 km in width. 52 mosques are spread out over the island including the most beautiful Ujra mosque. It has an ornately carved ceiling believed to be carved from a piece of driftwood.

The Lagoon is ideal for water sports, swimming and there are sandy beaches for sun basking. Enjoy marine life exhibits at the Marine Aquarium, and a vast collection of specimens at the Museum. View the exotic underwater world without getting yourself wet, from the glass-bottomed boats. Hire water sports crafts like Kayaks and Sailing Yachts.

Tourist Huts, white sandy beaches, colourful lagoon await you.

"Taratashi" package is ideal for a visit to Kavaratti. One can visit the island in Coral Reef Package also.

Kalpeni: Kalpeni has the largest lagoon among Lakshadweep islands. The lagoon is relatively shallow and ideal for all kinds of water sports. A peculiar feature of Kalpeni atoll is the huge storm bank of coral debris along the eastern and southeastern shoreline. Kalpeni with the small islets Tilakkam, Pitti and the uninhabited Cheriyam with sparkling lagoon in between them is known for its scenic beauty, Koomel, the gently curving bay offers tourists facilities like bath huts, change rooms etc. Besides swimming, tourists can engage themselves in water sports. Kayaks, Sail Boats, Pedal Boats are available on hire.

Apart from regular day tourists, the island can accommodate staying tourists in four tourist cottages managed privately by the islanders. The island is part of Coral Reef package.

Minicoy: This is the southern most island of the group, which is geographically isolated from other islands. Perhaps due to this, the culture here is a mix of Maldivian and South Indian. The language spoken is Mahl a form of Divehi, the language spoken in Maldives. It is a cousin of Indo-Persian languages whose script is written from right to left.

Minicoy, often called Women's Island for the dominating position enjoyed by ladies in the society. Here the village life has been democratic perhaps even before the words Democracy and Panchayat were known to them. It has a cluster of 10 villages each presided by a "Bodukaka". The island has a rich tradition of performing arts. Lava dance, the most attractive among them, is performed on festive occasions.

The island is a part of the Coral Reef package with facilities to accommodate staying tourists as well as day tourists. A new twenty-bedded tourist resort has started functioning. The island is included in the Swaying Palms package.

Kadmat: Kadmat is a haven of solitude with its fine lagoon of even depth, a long stretch of shoreline ideal for swimming and

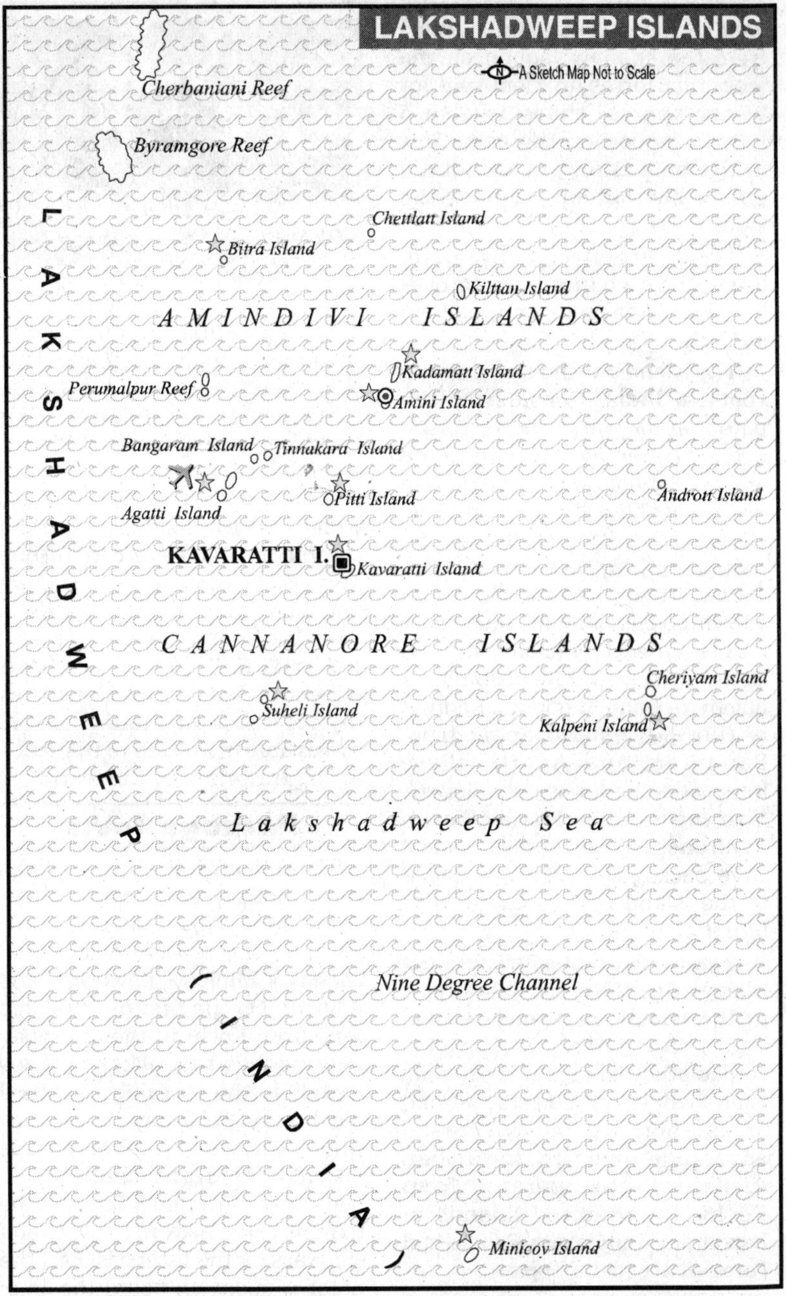

LAKSHADWEEP ISLANDS

❖ A Sketch Map Not to Scale

Cherbaniani Reef

Byramgore Reef

L
A
K
S
H
A
D
W
E
E
P

Chettlatt Island

☆ Bitra Island

Kilttan Island

A M I N D I V I   I S L A N D S

Kadamatt Island

Perumalpur Reef

Amini Island

Bangaram Island   Tinnakara Island

Agatti Island

Pitti Island

Andrott Island

KAVARATTI I.

Kavaratti Island

C A N N A N O R E   I S L A N D S

Cheriyam Island

Suheli Island

Kalpeni Island

L a k s h a d w e e p   S e a

Nine Degree Channel

I
N
D
I
A

Minicoy Island

129

well secluded tourist huts. Apart from the shallow lagoon on the west that forms an ideal spot for water sports, there is also a narrow lagoon on the east. This is the only island in the group which has lagoon on both the sides.

Thick green coconut palm leaves form a natural canopy over the whole area protecting you from sunlight.

The island has the finest diving spots in India. Considering the potential for water sports, a full-fledged Water Sports Institute and a Dive School with well-trained instructors have been set up in the island. Dive Package tours and regular staying package tours are arranged to the island. It can accommodate only 48 tourists at a time. Due to its exclusivity the island is increasingly becoming a haven for honeymooners. Kadmat is the only island apart from Bangaram and Agatti where international tourists are allowed. Visit the island in Marine Wealth Awareness Programme. Special Dive packages are also arranged to the island by M/s Laccadives, Mumbai, India.

Agatti: A virtual gateway to the islands, Agatti has the only airport in the island. A twenty-bedded tourist resort has been set up here. Unlike other islands it is the only island where one can stay as long or as short as one wishes-an advantage given by the Indian Airlines flight operated from Kochi. Uninhabited islands of Bangaram, Thinnakara, Parali-I and Parali-II are just a hop away.

Bangaram: A pleasure trip to an island that is uninhabited! The very idea unfurls several romantic thoughts. Bangaram is an island that does justice to all that romantic imaginations. This teardrop shaped piece of land is encircled by creamy sand. Even in the hottest part of the day, you won't feel the heat as luxuriant coconut trees shade you from Sun's rays. For a perfect outing, there are three uninhabited islands in the same atoll, Tinnakara, Parali-I and Parali-II. The deep, warm, clear waters of Indian Ocean with its myriad flora and fauna are an irresistible invitation to the scuba diving fraternity of the world.

Package Tours

Coral Reef: It is a five-day ship based holiday tour conducted on board M.V. Tipu Sultan. In this package the tourists visit three islands - Minicoy, Kavaratti, and Kalpeni. On the first day the ship sails from Kochi in the afternoon and reaches one of these three islands in the morning of second day around 8.00 a.m. In the day time tourists are taken to the islands for sight seeing, sea bathing etc. Around 5.00 p.m., the tourists come back to the ship and ship sails for the second island. The night is spent on board the ship.

Likewise three islands are visited and on the fifth day the ship reaches Kochi around 9.00 a.m.

Accommodation

M.V. Tipu Sultan has 4 deluxe class, 32 first class and 120 tourist class accommodations.

Cate-gory / Class	Adult/Child Transportation Cost (Rs.)	Adult Tour Package Cost (Rs.)
Deluxe class	10,000	5,000
First class	9,260	5,000
Tourist class	4,040	5,000

Students groups of 15 pax. and above are given a concessional rate. Accommodation in tourist class.

Those availing Deluxe class are accommodated in air-conditioned double berth cabins and First class tourists are accommodated in four berth air-conditioned cabins. Tourist class has an air-conditioned hall with push back seats.

Marine Wealth Awareness Programme: MWAP covers a 4-7 days package to Kadmat to experience the richness and beauty of marine life. The ship starts sailing from Kochi in the afternoon and reaches Kadmat the following day. Sea passage is by M.V. Tipu Sultan, M.V. Amindivi and M.V. Minicoy. This programme will be interesting to both water sports enthusiasts and leisure seekers.

Executive class tourists are accommodated in the air-conditioned cabins in the ship and air-conditioned cottages in the island. First class tourists will be accommodated in the air-conditioned cabins in the ship and non-AC cottages in the islands.

Accommodation

Category	Single/Night Cost (Rs.)	Double/Night Cost (Rs.)
A/C	2,500	4,000
Non A/C	2,000	3,000

Transportation

Category	Cost (both ways)
Deluxe class	Rs. 7,000/-
First class	Rs. 6,000/-
Tourist class	Rs. 3,500/-

Taratashi: A six-day package by ship to Paradise Island Huts, Kavaratti. The tourists sail from Kochi in the afternoon and reach Kavaratti the following day. Rest of the days is spent at Kavaratti. On the fifth day, they sail off from Kavaratti and reach Kochi around 9 a.m. on the sixth day. The stay on the island is in the tourist huts on the beach front. Tourists can enjoy swimming, scuba diving, snorkeling, water sports, lagoon cruise, glass bottomed boat cruise etc.

Accommodation

Category/ Class	Single/Night Cost (Rs.)	Double/Night Cost (Rs.)
Non A/C	1,500	3,000

Transportation

Category	Cost (both ways)
Deluxe class	Rs. 7,000/-
First class	Rs. 6,000/-
Tourist class	Rs. 3,500/-

Week end Tour Package to Kalpeni: Week end tour package is one day excursion package to Kalpeni island. On Saturday the ship departs from Kochi and on Monday morning ship returns to Kochi. Sunday will be spent with a range of water sports like snorkeling, kayaking, glass bottomed boat cruise etc.

Accommodation

Category/ Class	Trans (Rs.)	Package (Rs.)	Total (Rs.)
Adult A/C Chair	3000	1000	4000
Child A/C Chair	3000	500	350

Swaying Palm (Minicoy): 3-4 days' tour to Minicoy. Accommodation is arranged on the newly constructed 20 bedded tourist resort and private tourist cottages built on the beachfront. The light house built by British in 1885 is one of the attractions at Minicoy. Journey is by M.V. Tipu Sultan, M.V. Bharat seema and M.V. Minicoy and M.V. Amindivi.

Accommodation

Category	Single/Night Cost (Rs.)	Double/Night Cost (Rs.)
A/C	2,500	4,000
Non A/C	2,000	3,000

Scuba Diving Package: Scuba diving facilities are available at Kavaratti. Laccadives, Mumbai operates the scuba diving centres at Kadmat and Bangaram.

(a) Dive package for beginners :- Domestic tourists availing scuba diving package to Kadmat will be charged Rs.24,000/- per person for 8 days and for any additional day @ Rs.2,000/- Transportation charges extra depending on mode and class of transport.

(b) Dive package for advanced divers:- Domestic tourists availing this package will be charged Rs.2,000/- per day per person for accommodation. Dive charges and transportation will be extra.

Foreign nationals will be charged@US $75 per day per person. Dive extra.

All diving equipment will be provided. The minimum age to undergo the diving course is 14 years. All bookings are to be done one month in advance by sending 50% of the fee to : LACADIVES, E-20, Everest Building, Tardeo, Mumbai-400 034. ✆ : 91-22-66627381/82.Fax : 91-22-66669241.

Tourist Information Offices

- **KTDC,** Tourist Reception Centre, Shanmugham Road, Ernakulam, Cochin-31. ✆ : 9 1-484-2353234. Fax : 2382199
- **Asst. Gen. Manager - SPORTS,** Lakshadweep Office, Indira Gandhi Road, Willington Island, Kochi - 682 003. ✆: 91- 484-2668387, 2666789 Fax : 2668647.

Note : Service Tax applicable at prevailing Government tax rate for all the above packages.